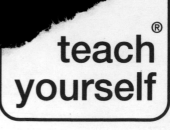

teach
yourself

beginner's
portuguese

D0432960

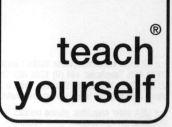

beginner's
portuguese
sue tyson-ward

Launched in 1938, the **teach yourself** series grew rapidly in response to the world's wartime needs. Loved and trusted by over 50 million readers, the series has continued to respond to society's changing interests and passions and now, 70 years on, includes over 500 titles, from Arabic and Beekeeping to Yoga and Zulu. What would you like to learn?

be where you want to be with **teach yourself**

ilton Park, Abingdon, Oxon
35 400454. Lines are open
answering service. Details
ourself.co.uk

ner Services, PO Box 545,
. Fax: 1-614-755-5645.

yerson Ltd, 300 Water St,
Fax: 905 430 5020.

Long renowned as the authoritative source for self-guided learning – with more than 50 million copies sold worldwide – the **teach yourself** series includes over 500 titles in the fields of languages, crafts, hobbies, business, computing and education.

British Library Cataloguing in Publication Data: a catalogue record for this title is available from the British Library.

Library of Congress Catalog Card Number: on file.

First published in UK 1996 by Hodder Education, part of Hachette Livre UK, 338 Euston Road, London, NW1 3BH.

First published in US 1996 by The McGraw-Hill Companies, Inc.

This edition published 2008.

The **teach yourself** name is a registered trade mark of Hodder Headline.

Typeset by Transet Limited, Coventry, England.
Printed in Great Britain for Hodder Education, an Hachette Livre UK Company, 338 Euston Road, London NW1 3BH, by CPI Cox & Wyman, Reading, Berkshire RG1 8EX.

The publisher has used its best endeavours to ensure that the URLs for external websites referred to in this book are correct and active at the time of going to press. However, the publisher and the author have no responsibility for the websites and can make no guarantee that a site will remain live or that the content will remain relevant, decent or appropriate.

Hachette Livre UK's policy is to use papers that are natural, renewable and recyclable products and made from wood grown in sustainable forests. The logging and manufacturing processes are expected to conform to the environmental regulations of the country of origin.

Impression number   10 9 8 7 6 5 4 3 2 1
Year   2012 2011 2010 2009 2008

contents

Dedication

For Mum and Dad

Acknowledgements

Many thanks to Mrs Brenda Wright, for her patient typing efforts, and to Mrs Maria Gilham for her valuable comments. For this new edition, thanks to Ginny Catmur and Alexandra Jaton at Hodder, for their careful editing, and guidance. Thanks, also, to Rosemary Morlin for her part in pulling the new edition together.

Teach Yourself Beginner's Portuguese is the right course for you if you are a complete beginner or wanting to make a fresh start. It is a self-study course which will help you to understand, read and speak most of the Portuguese you will need on holiday or a business trip.

The book has two parts. The first ten units introduce you to the basic structures and grammatical points you'll need in everyday situations. Units 1–10 should be taken in order as each builds on the previous one.

Units 11–19 deal with everyday situations such as shopping, eating, booking a room, travelling and give you the opportunity to put into practice the language you've acquired in the first part. These units may be taken in any order.

The course is best used together with the accompanying recording, but is not dependent upon it. You are recommended to obtain and use the recording if possible. The recorded dialogues and audio exercises indicated by the ▶ symbol give you plenty of practice in understanding the basic language; they will help you develop an authentic accent and increase your confidence in saying simple phrases. When you are learning a language, particularly in the early stages, there always seem to be long lists of words to wade through. Try to develop your own, efficient, ways of learning vocabulary. Stickers on items around the house, short lists of 'three words a day', memory techniques like mnemonics (visual prompts), making up rhymes, and learning words incorporated into phrases or sentences rather than as individual words out of context. Every person has their own way of learning and you must find the best way for you.

About Units 1–10

The first page tells you what you are going to learn. Then there is an easy exercise which gets you speaking straight away.

The **Vocabulary boxes** contain the most important words and phrases from the unit. Try to learn them by heart. They will be practised in the rest of the unit and the later units.

Diálogo *Dialogue*. Listen to the dialogues once or twice without stopping the recording or read through them without looking anything up; try to get the gist of them. The notes underneath each dialogue will help you to understand it. Then, using the pause button, break the dialogue into manageable chunks and try repeating each phrase out loud. This will help you acquire a more authentic accent.

Leitura *Reading* and **Monólogo** *Monologue*. Listen to these on your recording, checking you can get the gist of the passage first. Then make sure you know all the vocabulary.

Grammar. In this section, you may want to start by reading the example(s) then work out the grammatical point or you may prefer to read the **Grammar** first and see how the rule applies. Once you feel confident about a particular grammar point, try to create your own examples.

The **ℹ** section will help you understand the language by explaining differences due to cultural background and changes.

Exercises. Each activity, in this section, allows you to practise one of the points introduced in the **Grammar** section. In some activities you will need to listen to the recording. It is not essential to have the recording in order to complete this course, as most of the activities are not dependent on it. However, listening to the recording will make your learning much easier.

Self-evaluation. At the end of each unit you can test yourself on the last two or three unit(s).

About Units 11–19

The first page tells you what you are going to learn. You'll also find in many units a short text in Portuguese about the topic.

The **Vocabulary boxes** contain the basic vocabulary you'll need when coping, in real life, with practical situations such as checking into a hotel, ordering a snack, asking for a train timetable, going on an excursion.

Diálogos *Dialogues*. There are several short dialogues, each dealing with a different aspect of the topic. Remember to listen to the dialogues first and use pause to practise the new words and phrases out loud.

Exercises. The activities are mostly based on authentic Portuguese material. Here you can develop a feel for how things work in Portugal, as well as practising your reading skills. You will then have more confidence to cope with the real situations.

The **Testing yourself** section at the end of the book allows you to assess your progress. It is divided into two parts, covering Units 1–10 and 11–19.

Answers. The answers to the **Exercises, Documentos** and **Self-evaluations** can be found at the back of the book. Some listening exercises give you the answers on the recording.

Be successful at learning languages

1 **Do a little bit every day**, between 20 and 30 minutes if possible, rather than two or three hours in one session.
2 **Try to work towards short-term goals**: for example, work out how long you'll spend on a particular unit and work within this time limit.
3 **Revise and test yourself regularly** using the **Self-evaluation** at the end of each unit.
4 **Make use of the tips** given in the book and try to say the words and phrases out loud whenever possible.
5 **Try every opportunity to speak the language.** Attend some classes to practise your Portuguese with other people, get some help from a Portuguese speaker or find out about Portuguese clubs, societies, etc.
6 **Don't worry too much about making mistakes.** The important thing is to get your meaning across and remember that making mistakes in Portuguese will not stop a Portuguese person understanding you. Learning can be fun particularly when you find you can use what you have learnt in real situations.

At the back of the book

At the back of the book is a reference section which contains:

Key to the exercises, etc.
Portuguese–English vocabulary and **English–Portuguese vocabulary** lists containing all the main words in the course.

Numbers.
A **Grammar index** to enable you to look things up in the book.

Symbols and abbreviations

▶ This indicates that the recording is needed.

ℹ Cultural information.

(m) masculine
(f) feminine
(sing) singular
(pl) plural
(lit) literally

About the recording

Although this book can successfully be used on its own, the purchase of the recording will enhance both your pronunciation and your comprehension abilities as well as giving you the opportunity for aural revision.

▶ Pronunciation guide

Here is a simple guide to the letters of the alphabet, their Portuguese name [in brackets], and how to pronounce them:

A [á] ah	B [bê] bay	C [cê] say	D [dê] day	E [é] eh	F [éfe] eff
G [guê] gay	H [agá] ah-*gah*	I [i] ee	J [jota] *zhoh*-tah	K [capa] *cah*-pah	L [éle] el
M [éme] em	N [éne] en	O [ó] oh	P [pê] pay	Q [quê] kay	R [érre] air
S [ésse] ess	T [tê] tay	U [ú] oo	V [vê] vay	W [double vay] OR [dâblio]	X [xis] shish
Y [ípsilon OR I grego] eepsilon OR ee-*graygoo*	Z [zê] zay				

Although the letters K, W and Y do not appear in Portuguese words, the letters exist for use in foreign words and abbreviations. Listen to the whole alphabet on the recording a few times, then try to join in.

Most Portuguese words are pronounced as they are written – there are far fewer 'hidden' sounds or awkward sounds than in some other languages, such as English or French. Once you have de-coded a few tricky sounds, you should be able to have a go at reading Portuguese aloud as you see it. The following are some basic guidelines for some of the less straightforward pronunciation:

Portuguese letter/s	Pronunciation
ch	*sh*
lh	like the *lli* in *million*
nh	like the *ni* in *onion*
g, followed by e/i	like the *s* in plea*sure*
j	as above
h	always silent
x	tricky – varies from hard ks sound to a *z*, or even *sh*

Nasal sounds pronounced at the back of the nose are indicated by a ~ over the vowel, and also include words ending in -m or -n. Try to imagine saying them with a bad cold, when your nose is slightly blocked!

ão	*ow*
ãos	*owsh*
õe	*oy*
ões	*oysh*
ã	*ah*
ãs	*ahsh*
ãe	*eye*
ães	*eyesh*

One thing to remember is that when words run together when spoken, there is an effect on the ending and beginning of words involved, which may alter the sound from when a word is spoken in isolation from others. Also, regional variations, although fewer in Portugal than in some countries, do also alter sounds. The Algarve, in particular, is an area where the language can be difficult to work out at times.

The Portuguese alphabet is the same as the Roman one used in English, and other Latin-based languages.

- The only consonants you will find as a double are **rr** and **ss**
- A quick note here about the consonants **c**, **g** and **q**, which change their pronunciation depending on which vowels follow them. This can be a stumbling block for the uninitiated, hence a basic rule here:

  c before *a* / *o* / *u* = hard sound like *cat*

  ç (c + cedilla – see section on accents) before a/o/u = soft sound, like *face*

  c before *e* / *i* = soft

  g before *e* / *i* = soft, like the 's' sound in *treasure*

  g before *a* / *o* / *u* = hard, like in goal

  g + u before *e* / *i* = 'silent' *u* , e.g. **guitarra** *ghee* . . . NOT *gwee* . . .

  There are some exceptions (there always are!), such as **linguiça** (spicy sausage) = *lingwiça*.

  q is always followed by u

  qu before *e* / *i* = 'silent' u, e.g. **máquina** (machine) [*máKeena*, NOT *máKWeena*]; again there are some exceptions

  qu before *o* / *a* = *kw* e.g. **quadro** (picture) [*Kwadro*]
- **ph** does not exist in Portuguese: those words similar to English have an *f* – the same sound, but be careful with the spelling: e.g. **filósofo** = *philosopher*

Brazilian spelling

Despite many years of wrangling over spelling throughout the Portuguese-speaking world (and most particularly between Portugal and Brazil), up-to-date orthographic (spelling) agreements have still not been fully implemented. There are still some differences in spelling between the two variants of the language, mostly in the following areas, but even here not always consistently:

Common changes in consonants from European (EP) to Brazilian (BP) Portuguese

Spelling in EP	Example	Spelling in BP	Example
Words with a b in the middle	subtil	lose the *b*	sutil
cc and *cç*	secção	lose the first *c*	seção
mm, mn, nn	connosco comummente	become single *n* or *m*	conosco comumente
pç and *pt*	óptimo	lose the *p*	ótimo
ct	facto	lose the *c*	fato
t	registo	become *tr*	registro
gu/qu	cinquenta	*gü/qü*	cinqüenta
Numbers 16–19	dezasseis	change *a* to *e*	dezesseis

Accents

You will find the following written accents in Portuguese

´	Acute accent	Acento agudo	Opens vowel sound and indicates stress*	Gramática
^	Circumflex	Circunflexo	Closes vowel sound and indicates stress	português
~	Tilde	Til	Nasalizes vowel and usually indicates stress	amanhã
`	Grave accent	Acento grave	Opens vowel, non-stressing, indicates a contraction of two words	àquele

* Stress is the part of the word where you emphasise it when you say it.

There are also: ç c cedilha (cedilla), which makes the c soft, and as mentioned previously, the 'dieresis', ü, in gu and qu, to show they are pronounced as gw and qw.

Differences in Brazilian Portuguese

Some common changes to written accents are:

European	Brazilian
voo (no accent)	vôo (adds circumflex)
ténis (acute e accent)	tênis (becomes e circumflex)
abdómen (acute o)	abdômen (becomes o circumflex)
ideia (no accent)	idéia (adds acute accent)

Stress

Portuguese words are classified into three groups in terms of where the stress (emphasis) falls:

1 last syllable
2 penultimate (next to last)
3 antepenultimate

The majority belong to group 2 and do not usually require a written accent. The written accent occurs to enable words to be correctly stressed when they have deviated from the usual stress-pattern. Whenever you see a written accent, that is where you should emphasise the word when you say it. Words also carry a written stress mark to distinguish them from a word with the same spelling but a different meaning, e.g. **por** (by) and **pôr** (to put). These are relatively rare.

A few tips to help you acquire an authentic accent

It is not absolutely vital to acquire a perfect accent. The aim is to be understood; here are a number of techniques for working on your pronunciation:

1 Listen carefully to the recording or native speaker or teacher. Whenever possible repeat out loud imagining you are a native speaker of Portuguese.

2 Record yourself and compare your pronunciation with that of a native speaker.

3 Ask native speakers to listen to your pronunciation and tell you how to improve it.

4 Ask native speakers how a specific sound is formed. Watch them and practise at home in front of a mirror.

5 Make a list of words that give you pronunciation trouble and practise them.

▶ Now practise your pronunciation by saying these place names (if you have the recording listen to each one first), and look them up on the map, to see where each place is in Portugal.

First of all, the regions of Portugal:

1	Minho	6	Beira Baixa
2	Douro	7	Estremadura
3	Trás-os-Montes	8	Ribatejo
4	Beira Alta	9	Alentejo
5	Beira Litoral	10	Algarve

▶ And some main cities:

1	Lisboa	6	Porto
2	Faro	7	Braga
3	Guarda	8	Évora
4	Setúbal	9	Portalegre
5	Coimbra	10	Vila Real

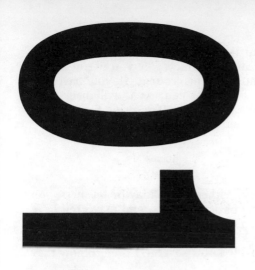

01

muito prazer
pleased to meet you

In this unit you will learn
- basic greetings
- how to ask and say how people are
- how to ask and give names
- common courtesies

Before you begin

Make sure you have read the introduction to the course and understood the tips for learning, which give you useful advice on how to make the most of this course. If you have the recording, use it as much as you can, as it will help your progress considerably. Repeat phrases often, using the pause to give you time to work at your own speed.

Exercise

If you have visited Portugal, either on holiday or business, you may well have heard some basic greetings, and may even have used some yourself. Try to think of a few words now and say them out loud, then check with the following list to see how you've got on – you probably know several. Listen to how they are pronounced on the CD.

▶
Bom dia.	*Good morning, hello.*
Boa tarde.	*Good afternoon, hello.*
Boa noite.	*Good evening (night), hello.*
Olá.	*Hi. (Hello.)*
Até logo.	*See you later.*
Até já.	*See you soon.*
Até amanhã.	*See you tomorrow.*
Até à próxima.	*See you next time.*
Tchau.	*Bye for now.*
Adeus.	*Goodbye.*

ℹ Portuguese greetings are less fixed to the time of day than the corresponding English phrases. **Bom dia** is used up until around 1.00 p.m., when many businesses close for lunch. **Boa tarde** is used during the afternoon and into the early evening. You will soon get an idea of when to use each greeting listening to Portuguese people during their day-to-day routines. The first three expressions above are also used as goodbye and are often accompanied by **adeus**, e.g. **adeus boa noite** and so on. **Tchau** is imported from Brazilian soap operas; it is very casual, as is **olá**.

▶ Diálogo 1

Paula meets a neighbour and briefly greets him.

Paula	Bom dia, senhor Mendes. Como está?
Sr Mendes	Estou bem, obrigado, e a senhora?
Paula	Bem, obrigada.

Paula sees an acquaintance, Ana, approaching.

▶ **Paula**   Olá, Ana, está boa?
Ana   Estou, e a Paula?
Paula   Também estou, obrigada.
Ana   Então, até já.
Paula   Adeus, até logo.

como está?	*how are you?*
estou bem	*I'm well*
obrigado	*thank you* (said *by males*)
está boa?	*are you well? lit. are you good? (to a woman)*
e	*and*
também	*also*
obrigada	*thank you* (said *by females*)
então	*well then / right then*

Grammar

1 'Thank you'

In this first dialogue you met **obrigado** and **obrigada**, both meaning *thank you*. **Obrigado** is used by men and **obrigada** by women: these are the masculine and feminine forms of the same word.

Many words in Portuguese are divided into male and female forms; this comes from Latin, the base of the Portuguese language. If you know a bit of any other Latin-based language, such as French, this concept will not be new to you. If you don't, don't worry; there will be plenty of opportunities to get used to the two versions of the same word. In Portuguese, the ending of words shows whether that word is masculine (usually an -o ending), or feminine (usually -a). You will learn more about this as you go along.

2 'You'

The Portuguese use a different word for *you* depending on how well they know the person, whether the person is in a higher social position, has senior work status, if they are older, and so on. In the dialogue you met two of the more formal words meaning *you*.

o senhor (male)	*you* lit. *the gentleman / sir*
a senhora (female)	*you* lit. *the lady / madam*

The other *you* you have met is **o** or **a** + the name of the person:

o Miguel   *you (to Miguel,* masculine)
a Paula   *you (to Paula,* feminine)

This is often used between colleagues or by older people to younger people.

You will learn more of these varied forms as you go along.

3 I am, you are: to be

In the dialogue, people were asking and saying how they are, using:

estou   *I am*
está   *you are*

In English, *to be* is known as the infinitive of the verb. In Portuguese the equivalent infinitive is **estar**. (This is the form of the verb you will find in a dictionary.)

The verb **estar**, *to be*, is used to describe temporary feelings, states, characteristics and places.

4 Questions

In Portuguese, you can ask a simple question by raising your voice at the end of a sentence. There is usually no change in word-order, as is often the case in English questions.

Como está?   *How are you?* (lit. *how you are?*)
Está boa.   *You are well (said to a woman).*
Está boa?   *Are you well ?* (lit. *you are good?*)

Exercises

1   Fill in the gaps in this dialogue.

Ana   Boa noite, senhor Silva. Como . . . . . ?
Sr Silva   . . . . . bem, obrigado. E a senhora?
Ana   Estou . . . , ...
Sr Silva   Então, boa . . . . . e . . . amanhã.
Ana   . . . noite.

2   What would you say to these people in the following situations?

   a   meeting your friend Ana Paula mid-morning.
   b   bumping into a business colleague at lunch time.

c leaving a group of friends mid-afternoon – and you'll be seeing them again tomorrow.
d popping into town to go shopping – you'll see your family later.
e meeting your teacher in the evening.

Documento

At what part of the day is this programme broadcast?

> **JORNAL DA TARDE**
>
> Telejornal nacional e internacional; o tempo.

▶ Diálogo 2

Nuno asks Paula to a party, where she meets some people her age.

Nuno	Boa noite, Miguel, estás bom?
Miguel	Estou, e tu?
Nuno	Estou óptimo, obrigado.
Miguel	(*turning to Paula*) Desculpa, como te chamas?
Paula	Chamo-me Paula, e tu?
Miguel	Miguel.
Paula	Muito prazer.
Miguel	Igualmente.

desculpa	*excuse me*
chamo-me	*I am called / my name is*
estás bom?	*are you well? (to a man)*
estou óptimo/a	*I'm really well / fine*
muito prazer	*pleased to meet you*
igualmente	*likewise*

i The Portuguese, although more reserved than the Spanish, are generally tactile; it is common when you greet someone to shake hands, slap each other's backs, or kiss on each cheek. Obviously if you are meeting people for the first time take your cue from their behaviour towards you – if you are too informal you may offend.

Grammar

1 Informal 'you'

In Dialogue 2, the friends addressed each other by **tu**, which is
the informal form of *you* – for friends, family and young people.
The verb form also changed from **está** to **estás**.

| está | *you are* (more formal) |
| estás | *you are* (informal) |

2 Chamo-me . . . *My name is . . .*

You will have noticed that when Paula was asked **Como *te*
chamas?**, she responded with **chamo-*me***. Don't worry at this
stage about the varied position of the words **te** and **me**. Note
that when asking the name of someone older, or whom you do
not know very well, you use **como *se* chama?**, which is more
formal.

3 Desculpa *Excuse me*

The word **desculpa** (or **desculpe** when used with strangers) can
be used to mean *I'm sorry* in situations such as in Dialogue 2,
as well as when interrupting a conversation, on approaching
someone in the street to ask a question, or for apologizing if you
have bumped into someone. You will also hear:

| perdão | *sorry / I beg your pardon* |
| com licença | *excuse me* (if you want to pass by) |

Possible responses include:

| não faz mal | *don't worry* |
| com certeza / faz favor | *of course / go ahead* |

Exercises

▶ **3 Actividade três:** You have just met Nuno in the street.
Complete your conversation in Portuguese following the
English prompts.

	Nuno	Boa tarde, como está?
a	**You**	*Say hello. Tell him you're fine, thanks. Ask him how he is.*
	Nuno	Estou bem, obrigado.
b	**You**	*Say goodbye. Tell him you'll see him tomorrow.*
	Nuno	Então, até à próxima.

4 What would you say to these people to find out their names?

a Ana Maria   **b** José   **c** Senhor Mendes

5 The expressions for six greetings (*hello / goodbye*) are hidden in this wordsearch. The words run across, down, up, backwards and diagonally.

K	O	B	D	L	G	S	E
M	T	A	Z	P	O	D	O
A	S	J	D	H	R	W	F
I	L	E	N	A	P	J	C
D	A	T	T	D	O	R	Q
M	J	A	F	E	A	Z	S
O	O	R	K	U	B	C	Y
B	S	C	T	S	E	F	P
O	G	O	L	E	T	A	D
C	T	S	B	R	O	L	A

6 The following dialogue has become mixed up. Can you unscramble it? To help you get started the first line is **Bom dia, como está?**

Lúcia	Bem, obrigada.
Sr Silva	Eduardo.
Lúcia	Bom dia, como está?
Lúcia	Chamo-me Lúcia, e o senhor?
Sr Silva	Estou bem, obrigado, e a senhora?
Sr Silva	Igualmente.
Lúcia	Muito prazer.
Sr Silva	Desculpe, como se chama?

Parabéns! (*Well done!*) You have completed the first unit. Now try this **Self-evaluation** to see what you have learnt.

Self-evaluation

Now check you can:

a say 'good afternoon' and ask someone (formally) how they are.
b say 'goodnight' and 'see you next time'.
c ask someone their name (informally).
d give your name.
e apologize for stepping on someone's foot!
f say you're pleased to meet someone.

02

de onde é?

where are you from?

In this unit you will learn
- how to ask where people are from
- how to say where you are from
- how to talk about nationalities

Before you begin

Different people have different ways of learning but most people would agree that studying for 20 minutes regularly is better than occasionally spending two hours in one go. Listen to the dialogues once or twice without the book (or read them out loud if you haven't got the recording). Then go through the new words one by one.

▶ Diálogo 1

A group of people have just met at a party. They are finding out where each other comes from.

Sr Pereira   Boa noite. Chamo-me Rui Pereira. E como se chama a senhora?
Isabel   Isabel.
Sr Pereira   Muito prazer, Isabel. De onde é?
Isabel   Sou inglesa; sou de Londres. E o senhor, de onde é?
Sr Pereira   Sou português, sou de Lisboa.

de onde é?	*where are you from?*
sou	*I am*
inglesa	*English (woman)*
sou de	*I am from*
Londres	*London*
português	*Portuguese (man)*
Lisboa	*Lisbon*

▶ Diálogo 2

Senhor Pereira asks a couple where they come from.

Sr Pereira   Boa noite. De onde são os senhores?
Susana   Somos da Espanha. Somos espanhóis.
Mário   A Susana é de Madrid, e eu sou de Barcelona. E o senhor, de onde é?
Sr Pereira   Pois, sou de Portugal!

de onde são?	*where are you from?*
os senhores	*you (polite, plural form)*
somos	*we are*
Espanha	*Spain*
espanhóis	*Spanish (people)*

é	is
eu	I
pois	well

Grammar

1 More about 'to be'

In the previous unit, you learnt **está** *you are* and **estou** *I am*, to talk about how people are feeling. These current dialogues introduce you to another Portuguese verb **ser** *to be*; it is generally used to describe more permanent characteristics, such as your nationality and where you come from.

Sou de Portugal.	*I am from Portugal.*
De onde **é**?	*Where are you from?*
Susana **é** de Madrid.	*Susan is from Madrid.*
Somos da Espanha.	*We are from Spain.*
De onde **são**?	*Where are you* (pl) *from?*

2 I, you, he, she, we ...

This set of words (personal pronouns) indicates who is *in play* at any time, (who is the subject of the verb). But these words are rarely used in Portuguese, because the ending of the verb (the action word) shows the person in question:

sou	*I am*
eu sou	*I am*

The personal pronoun is useful for giving emphasis (*I'm from Spain*), or when a particular verb ending may indicate one of a choice of people (**é** = *you are, she / he / it is*). You will learn more about verbs later. The full set of personal pronouns is:

Singular		Plural	
eu	I	**nós**	We
tu	You (informal)	**vós**	You (outdated, rarely used)
ele	He/it	**eles**	They (m)
elas	She/it	**elas**	They (f)
o senhor (m)/ **a senhora** (f)	You (polite, formal)	**os senhores** (mpl)/ **as senhoras** (fpl)	You (polite, formal)
você	You (semi-formal)	**vocês**	You plural

3 Nationality

In Unit 1 you learnt that certain words in Portuguese have either a masculine or feminine ending, depending on whom (or what) that word is referring to. The same is true of words describing people's nationality. Also, if you are talking about more than one person, you must remember to change the word into a plural one. This sounds rather complex, but in fact, once you have got used to the idea, it is very logical, and with practice it becomes second nature.

Have a look at this table and compare the singular and plural forms of the nationalities:

Nationality

Name of country	Masculine singular	Feminine singular	Masculine plural	Feminine plural
A Itália *Italy*	italiano	italianos	italiana	italianas
Os Estados Unidos *USA*	americano	americanos	americana	americanas
O Brasil *Brazil*	brasileiro	brasileiros	brasileira	brasileiras
A Grécia *Greece*	grego	gregos	grega	gregas
A Austrália *Australia*	australiano	australianos	australiana	australianas
A Inglaterra *England*	inglês	ingleses	inglesa	inglesas
Portugal	português	portugueses	portuguesa	portuguesas
A Irlanda (do norte) *Northern Ireland*	irlandês	irlandeses	irlandesa	irlandesas
A França *France*	francês	franceses	francesa	francesas
A Escócia *Scotland*	escocês	escoceses	escocesa	escocesas
A China *China*	chinês	chineses	chinesa	chinesas
A Alemanha *Germany*	alemão	alemães	alemã	alemãs
A Espanha *Spain*	espanhol	espanhóis	espanhola	espanholas

If you have two or more males, you will use the masculine plural, similarly, a group of women will need the feminine plural. However, should you have a mixed group, the masculine plural is applied, even if your group consists of 100 women and just one man!

Notice that the names of countries can be masculine (o) or feminine (a). Some countries, such as Portugal itself, do not use this structure. This is just an anomaly in the language – you have to get used to them! The USA is plural (os), as it refers to the group of states.

O Brasil	(*Brazil*)
A Itália	(*Italy*)
Os Estados Unidos	(*United States*)
Sou alemã	*I am German* (f.)
É inglês?	*Are you English?*
Tom é escocês	*Tom is Scottish*

Exercises

1 Check with the nationalities table on page 22 and do the following:

    a Say which country you are from.
    b Give your nationality.
    c Ask Senhor Silva where he's from.
    d Say that Ana is Brazilian.
    e Ask Mr and Mrs Brito where they are from.
    f Say that Paulo is from Italy.
    g Say that the McDonalds are Scottish.

2 Fill in the spaces in the speech bubbles of the following people, who are talking about their nationalities and where they are from.

a

Maria

O sr / a sra Schmidt

Ellen / Mary

Sandra, John, Brenda

Marco Giovanni

Mac

3 Now write sentences about the same people a, b, c, d, e, f, using the correct part of ser (to be). It is common practice in Portugal to use o (masculine) / a (feminine) before people's names, hence the first example would read:

A Maria é de Portugal. *Maria is from Portugal.*
  É portuguesa. *She is Portuguese.*

You could use the word for *she* (ela) here, for emphasis.

Ela é portuguesa.

Now try the rest. You could use *he* (ele) and *they* (eles masculine, elas feminine).

▶ Diálogo 3

David has just met someone and he is trying to start a conversation.

David Bom dia. Desculpe, mas fala inglês?
João Não, não falo. O senhor é inglês?
David Sim, sou. Falo um pouco de português. Mas, o senhor é português?
João Não, não sou.
David Mas fala bem português.
João Sou brasileiro!

mas	*but*	**falo**	*I speak*
fala ...?	*do you speak ...?*	**um pouco de**	*a bit of*
não	*no / not*	**bem**	*well*
sim	*yes*		

Grammar

1 Saying 'yes' and 'no'

To say something negative, you place the word **não** before the verb:

não sou.	*I am not.*
não falo.	*I do not speak.*

Note there is no Portuguese equivalent of the word *do* in this second sentence. On answering a question, you will hear the double negative, as in the dialogue: **não, não falo** – *no, I do **not** speak*.

The word for *yes* is **sim**. Both of these words are nasalized – i.e. they should be pronounced like many French words, at the back of the nose. This takes some practice for English speakers, so keep trying! See the **Pronunciation guide** for more on this.

2 Languages

The name of a language is the same as the male nationality, hence **italiano** can mean the *Italian language*, or an *Italian man*. A German woman could say:

Sou alemã, falo alemão.	*I'm German (a German woman), I speak German.*

i As Portuguese is a language spoken in many continents, from South America, across Africa, and into Asia, as well as in Continental Portugal (including Madeira and the Azores), you may well meet various speakers of the language on your travels. Brazil, of course, has an enormous number of Portuguese speakers, and Brazilian soap operas are extremely popular in Portugal. The differences between Brazilian and European Portuguese are roughly akin to those between American and British English on pronunciation, vocabulary, and some points of grammar. In Dialogue 3 João was Brazilian. Did you notice his different accent?

Exercises

4 How would you do the following?

a Ask someone if they speak Italian.
b Say you are not American.
c Say you speak Portuguese and English.
d Ask someone if they speak Portuguese.
e Say you are not German, but you speak German.

5 Decide whether these statements about which languages people speak is true (V=verdadeiro) or false (F=falso). Assume each one only speaks the native language of their country!

a A Sara é dos Estados Unidos. Fala alemão.
b O Marco fala italiano; é da Itália.
c Eu sou do Brasil, falo português.
d A senhora Gomes é da Escócia. Fala inglês.
e O senhor Mendes fala alemão. É português.

Documento 1

a Which language is the most widely spoken?
b Which are the last two on the table?

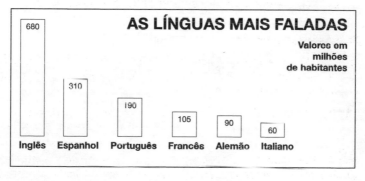

AS LÍNGUAS MAIS FALADAS

Valores em milhões de habitantes

680	310	190	105	90	60
Inglês	Espanhol	Português	Francês	Alemão	Italiano

▶ 6 **Actividade seis:** An interviewer (**entrevistador**) is doing a questionnaire about languages and nationalities. You decide to participate. Follow the prompts to help you complete the dialogue.

Entrevistador Boa tarde. Desculpe, mas fala português?
a You *Say yes, you speak a little bit.*
Entrevistador É da Alemanha?
b You *Say no, you're not German, and give your nationality.*

Entrevistador	Então (well then), fala inglês?
c You	*Say yes, you speak English, and also Italian.*
Entrevistador	Fala bem português.
d You	*Say thank you, and goodbye.*

Documento 2

Which languages are spoken at this shop?

AQUI FALA-SE
INGLÊS,
PORTUGUÊS,
ALEMÃO

Self-evaluation

a Ask Paulo where he's from.
b Say which country you are from.
c Ask Senhor Mendes if he is Brazilian.
d Ask where Mr and Mrs Oliveira come from.
e Speak on behalf of yourself and a friend, giving your nationality.
f Say that Júlia is Portuguese.
g Ask if João is from the USA.
h Ask someone if they speak English.
i Say no, you don't speak German.
j Say yes, you are English.

03 onde mora?
where do you live?

In this unit you will learn
- how to talk about where you live
- how to talk about addresses
- how to talk about where you work
- how to ask other people about where they live and work
- numbers 0–20

Before you begin

There is a variety of situations in which you may have to talk about where people live; it could be an informal conversation, or you may be filling in forms (at the bank, for example), or you may need someone's address in order to pay them a visit. There are, in fact, two verbs in Portuguese, which can be used to mean to live: **morar** and **viver**. **Morar** has close associations with **morada** meaning address, and **viver** with a larger scale, such as one's country, but, nowadays, you will hear both verbs equally. The dialogues in this unit will give you examples in each verb.

▶ Diálogo 1

Ana is finding out where different people live. Read and listen to the dialogue below.

Ana	Boa noite, senhor Mendes. Onde mora?
Sr Mendes	Moro em Lisboa, na Avenida da República. E a Ana, mora em Lisboa?
Ana	Não, moro aqui em Albufeira. Onde moram o senhor e a senhora Silva?
Sr Mendes	Moram no Porto, na Praça São Vicente. Onde mora o José?
Ana	O José? Pois, agora vive no Brasil.

mora	*you live, he, she lives*
moro	*I live*
em	*in*
na	*on / in (the)*
(a) avenida	*(the) avenue*
a Avenida da República	*(the) Republic Avenue*
aqui	*here*
moram	*they live, you* (pl) *live*
(a) praça	*(the) square*
agora	*now*
vive	*he / she lives, you live*

Grammar

1 How to say 'the'

You have already learnt about the idea of masculine and feminine words, and you have seen the words **o** and **a** (yes, they may be only one letter, but they are in fact words!) used with certain countries, and with people's names. In the dialogue above, there are examples of these words used to describe where people live:

a avenida	*the avenue*
a praça	*the square*

Everything – that is all objects, people, animals, concepts – in the Portuguese language are either masculine or feminine. Most masculine words end in -o, and most feminine ones, like the examples above, end in -a. Likewise the words for *the* are **o** for masculine words, and **a** for feminine words. As you progress you will find many words do not fit the -o/-a ending structure, so you will have to learn from the vocabulary box which group they belong to. To form the plural *the*, (i.e. when talking about more than one object) just add an -s to the appropriate form.

as avenidas   *the avenues*

Wherever helpful, words will be identified with the **o** or **a**, or (m) or (f) in the vocabulary boxes in the rest of this course.

2 How to say 'in' and 'on'

The word for describing *in* or *on*, is **em**, as seen in **moro** *em* Lisboa. However, when you follow this word by any of the words for *the*, the words join together; usually when this happens, it is to help pronunciation, as some combinations of sounds would otherwise be rather awkward. So, the combinations, or contractions, are as follows:

- em + o/a   =   no / na
  in + the (masculine / feminine)=   *in / on the*

  em + a praça
  na praça   =   *in the square*

and in the plural,

- em + os/as   =   nos, nas
  em + as avenidas
  nas avenidas   =   *in the avenues*

3 Forming verbs

Up to now, you have been using parts of the two verbs **ser/estar** *to be* to talk about different aspects of people. You learnt in Unit 2 how to use the verb **falar** *to speak* and now you have been introduced to the verbs **morar / viver** *to live*. Many verbs follow the same pattern of endings as **falar**, as the -**ar** ending is the most common in Portuguese. Compare **falar, morar** and **trabalhar** (*to work*) which you will use later in this chapter:

falar *to speak*		**morar** *to live*	
fal*o*	I speak	**mor***o*	I live
fal*as*	you speak (informal)	**mor***as*	you live (informal)
fal*a*	he, she speaks / you speak	**mor***a*	he, she lives / you live
fal*amos*	we speak	**mor***amos*	we live
fal*am*	they speak / you (pl) speak	**mor***am*	they live / you (pl) live

trabalhar *to work*	
trabalh*o*	I work
trabalh*as*	you work (informal)
trabalh*a*	he, she works / you work
trabalh*amos*	we work
trabalh*am*	they work / you (pl) work

Can you spot the similar patterns? It is the continued presence of the letter **a**, brought down from the initial -**ar** ending.

Verbs are a complex part of any language, so you will need to take your time to get used to them. Don't worry if you get things wrong to begin with, the important thing is to have a go.

Exercises

1 So, now have a go. How do you do the following?

   a Ask senhora Gomes where she lives.
   b Say that you live in England.
   c Say that Maria lives in the square.
   d Ask where senhor and senhora Neto live.
   e Ask Renato if he lives in Germany.

2 Match up the people on the left with a correct part of the verb **morar** and the correct part of **no/na** (*in / on the*) to fit the place they live.

	Eu (*I*) —	moro mora moram	no na nos nas	praça

a	Lúcia (*she*)	moramos	nas	avenida.
b	Nós (*we*)	mora	no	rua (*street*).
c	(*you*)	moro	na	beco (*alley*).
d	Eles (*they*)	moram	nos	praça.

▶ Leitura *Reading*

Listen to and follow the passage below, in which João is giving his address to someone, and describing exactly where he lives.

Moro em Silves no Algarve, na Rua Samora Barros, número seis, e o apartamento fica no terceiro andar, à esquerda.

Now listen to and read about where Marília lives:

Eu vivo em Portugal, em Lisboa. Vivo numa casa antiga na Praça de Camões, número quinze, segundo andar, à direita.

(o) número	number
o apartamento	the apartment, flat
fica	is situated
(o) terceiro	third
(o) andar	floor
à esquerda	on the left
numa casa antiga	in an old house
(o) segundo	second
à direita	on the right

Grammar

▶ 1 Os números *Numbers*

You cannot get very far without numbers, in any language, as they creep into so many daily transactions – addresses, time, money, quantities – so you must start now to build up a good grasp of them. Let's start with 0–20. Listen to the numbers and repeat them out loud before you look at them. Say them every day for at least a week, and test yourself by counting backwards, or asking someone to test you out loud.

0	zero	11	onze
1	um, uma	12	doze
2	dois, duas	13	treze
3	três	14	catorze
4	quatro	15	quinze
5	cinco	16	dezasseis
6	seis	17	dezassete
7	sete	18	dezoito
8	oito	19	dezanove
9	nove	20	vinte
10	dez		

Numbers *one* and *two* have both a masculine and a feminine form – so if you are talking about two houses, **duas** cas<u>as</u>.

▶ 2 1st, 2nd, 3rd ...

primeiro	1st	quarto	4th
segundo	2nd	quinto	5th
terceiro	3rd		

You will learn further ones as you go along. If you are talking about anything feminine, then the final -o must change to an -a:

a terceir**a** cas**a**   *the third house*

These words are not only used for talking about floors in a building, you will also find them in Unit 11 on directions, and Unit 7 on days of the week.

3 How to say 'a' or 'an'

The words for number *one* are also the masculine and feminine forms of the words for *a* (*an*). Therefore, you can talk in terms of **uma casa** *a house* or **um apartamento** *an apartment*. Remember always to check in the vocabulary lists to see whether the word is masculine or feminine. This is referred to as the word's gender. If you are using a dictionary, then the word will usually be followed by (m) or (f). If there is no indication of gender, it is because the word belongs to the standard -o/-a ending.

4 How to say 'in a' or 'on a'

In the reading, you came across the expression **vivo _numa_ casa antiga** (_I live in an old house_). This is another example of a contracted structure, just like the **no/na** you learnt in Unit 2. Here you have: **em + um/uma**, becoming **num** and **numa**. Again, it makes it easier to say: try saying **em um** – it is very awkward.

5 Words for describing

Words that describe things (adjectives), such as **antigo** (_old_), are usually placed after the word they are describing. They also have to have the same appropriate masculine or feminine ending, and must be either singular or plural. This is called agreeing. Therefore a modern apartment would be **um apartamento moderno,** and two old houses would be **duas casas antigas.** You will learn more of these words in the next unit.

Exercise

3 The following people have got lost. Look at the descriptions they give of where they live, and match them up with the address plates:

a.

Praça de S.Jorge
Nº 6

i

Moro num apartamento moderno numa praça. Fica no terceiro andar, à direita.

b.

Rua do Ouro
Nº 11

ii

Moro na Rua do Ouro, número dezasseis, segundo andar.

i You may have noticed an abbreviation on the address plates above, regarding the number of the floor people live on – 3°, 2° and so on meaning third, second. Other common address abbreviations to look out for are R. (rua), r/c (rés-do-chão = *ground floor*), Av. (avenida), Pr. (praça), esq. (esquerda), dir. (direita). Many streets are named after famous historical or military heroes, or dates of historical events, such as 25 de Abril (*25th April* – when the 1974 revolution took place), or Praça de Camões (named after Portugal's national poet).

Documento

Look at the two address cards and decide which place belongs to senhor Mendes, whose establishment is on the ground floor, on a street.

Aberto das 7:30 às 21:30h. Encerra ao Sábado.
Rua Dr. Augusto E. Nunes, 40 r/c • Tel. 29698

Café-Restaurante **O AVENIDA**

• **Cozinha Regional**
• **Petiscos**
• **Com nova sala de refeições**

Aberto das 7 às 23h. Encerra aos Domingos.

Av. São Sebastião, 25 • Tel. 33872

▶ Diálogo 2

Paulo and Maria are talking about where they work.

Paulo	Maria, onde é que trabalha?
Maria	Trabalho em Faro, no aeroporto.
Paulo	E o que faz?
Maria	Trabalho no check-in. E o Paulo, onde trabalha?
Paulo	Sou banqueiro; trabalho num banco em Tavira.

onde trabalha?	*where do you work?*
onde é que trabalha?	*where is it that you work?*
trabalho	*I work*
o que faz?	*what do you do?*

Now, could you work out where they work? Have a look again at what they say, and see if you can find any connections with English words. Maria works at Faro airport, at the check-in desk, and Paulo is a bank clerk in a bank in Tavira.

Grammar

1 Onde (é que) . . .? *Where (is it that) . . . ?*

You will often hear Portuguese people inserting the expression **é que** into questions, usually to pad out what they are saying. So you could say **onde é que mora?** (**onde mora?**) as well as **onde é que trabalha?** (**onde trabalha?**).

2 Professions

When someone asks you **onde trabalha?**, or **o que faz?**, there are two ways you can answer, as Maria and Paulo did in the dialogue. You can either say **trabalho em . . .** *I work in* or **sou . . .** *I am . . .* When you are describing your place of work, don't forget the contractions **num, numa, no** and **na**.

So, you could say:

Trabalho num banco	*I work in a bank*
Trabalho numa escola	*in a school*
Trabalho num escritório	*in an office*
Trabalho numa empresa	*in a business*
Trabalho na universidade	*in the university*

Trabalho no banco Espírito Santo	*in the Espírito Santo bank*

Or,

Sou professor / professora	*I am a teacher*
Sou estudante	*student*
Sou escritor / escritora	*writer*
Sou médico / médica	*doctor*
Sou enfermeiro / enfermeira	*nurse*
Sou advogado / advogada	*lawyer*

You may be a **dona de casa** (*housewife*) or a **homem / mulher de negócios** (*businessman/woman*), or you may not work, **não trabalho, estou reformado/a** (*I do not work, I'm retired*), **estou desempregado/a** (*I'm unemployed*).

With names of professions, the Portuguese do not use the word *a*, they say literally *I am teacher*.

Exercises

4 Try these.

   a Ask senhor Gomes where he works.
   b Say that you are a student.
   c Ask José what he does for a living.
   d Say where you work.
   e Say that you do not work.

5 Complete the sums, choosing from the words in the list on the right-hand side.

   a Dois + três   = —— treze
   b Vinte – oito   = —— dezanove
   c Dezassete – quatro   = —— dezoito
   d Nove + nove   = —— cinco
   e Dez – oito   = —— dois
   f Quinze + quatro   = —— doze

6   Work out where these people work and fill in the locations
    in the grid below.

  a   Sou estudante.
  b   Sou banqueiro.
  c   Sou mulher de negócios.
  d   Trabalho no check-in.
  e   Sou secretária.
  f   Sou professora.

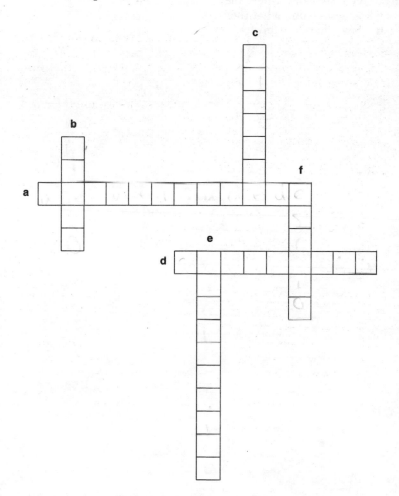

Self-evaluation

Check if you can now do the following:

a Count up to 20, forwards and backwards – out loud.
b Ask where Mr and Mrs Pereira live.
c Say where you live.
d Describe the location of your house.
e Say that you live in a modern house.
f Ask someone where they work.
g Ask someone what they do.
h Say what your profession is.
i Say where you work.

04

a família

the family

In this unit you will learn
- how to point people out
- how to describe your family
- how to talk about age

Before you begin

Before learning a second verb meaning *to be* in this unit, look back at Unit 2 to make sure you can say *I am* and *you are*.

▶ Diálogo 1

Senhor Moura is pointing out his family to a friend while at a party.

Alexandra	Boa tarde, Senhor Moura. Está cá sozinho?
Sr Moura	Não, estou com a minha família. Este é o meu filho Roberto, e esta é a minha filha mais velha, Sônia.
Alexandra	Muito prazer. E a senhora Moura?
Sr Moura	Pois, a minha mulher é aquela senhora ali.
Alexandra	E quem é aquele senhor ali?
Sr Moura	É o nosso chefe!

cá	*here*
sozinho	*alone*
com	*with*
a minha família	*my family*
este (m)	*this*
o meu filho	*my son*
esta (f)	*this*
a minha filha	*my daughter*
mais velha	*eldest*
a minha mulher	*my wife*
aquela (f)	*that*
ali	*there, over there*
quem?	*who?*
aquele (m)	*that*
o nosso chefe	*our boss*

ℹ️ There are two words for *wife* in Portuguese; **a mulher**, as in the dialogue, and also **a esposa**. The latter seems to be considered more polite, if you were asking after someone's wife, **como está a sua esposa?**, and the former tends to be used more when talking about one's own wife. When in doubt, take your cue from what Portuguese people are saying around you as expressions, like fashions, come and go.

Grammar

1 Este / aquele *This / that*

You should have noticed the different words used in the dialogue for pointing out people. **Este** (m) / **esta** (f) is used for people, or things near to you, and **aquele** (m) / **aquela** (f) for those at a distance. To talk about more than one person or thing, just add an -s, to make the plurals *these* and *those*.

este	esta	estes	estas	*this / these*
aquele	aquela	aqueles	aquelas	*that / those*

aquelas senhoras	*those women*
estes senhores	*these men*

2 O meu / o nosso *My / our*

When talking about a possession (this includes family members) you must make sure that the word you use for *my, your* and so on agrees (matches) with the object in possession. This can sometimes be awkward to grasp, but it should help you to remember that these words are **describing** possession in some way, and that, as you have already learnt in Unit 2, descriptive words (adjectives) agree with the word they are describing. Even though you may be a man talking about your daughter, you would use the feminine word for *my*. Here are some of the possessive words you are going to need:

	masculine word	feminine word
my	o meu	a minha
your (singular, polite)	o seu	a sua
our	o nosso	a nossa

To talk about more than one possessed object (i.e. in the plural), add an -s to the appropriate word.

a<u>s</u> nossa<u>s</u> filha<u>s</u>	*our daughters*

Did you notice in each case the word for the (**o, a, os, as**) is included? So what you actually end up saying is *the my*, and so on. This is just a quirk of the language – don't worry, all languages are full of them!

3 Mais ou menos *More or less*

When describing someone who is older, younger, taller, smaller, etc. you need the words **mais** (*more*) and **menos** (*less*) used with the appropriate adjective. So you can have combinations such as:

mais velho	*older*	o mais velho	*the oldest*
mais novo	*younger*	o mais novo	*the youngest*
mais alto	*taller*	o mais alto	*the tallest*
mais baixo ⎫	*shorter*	o mais baixo	*the shortest*
menos alto ⎭			

Don't forget to make the adjectives agree. A girl who is younger will be **mais nova,** and boys who are the tallest will be **os mais altos.** The words should appear after the person or thing they refer to:

o filho mais alto	*the tallest son*
as senhoras mais velhas	*the oldest ladies*

Exercises

1   Use the box of family members to help you complete these sentences following the guide in brackets.

o filho	son	**o irmão**	brother
a filha	daughter	**a irmã**	sister
o marido	husband	**o pai**	father
a mulher	wife	**a mãe**	mother

The plural of **filho** – **filhos** – can mean *sons,* or *children.*

a   Este é (*my brother*) _____ .
b   Aquela é (*our mother*) _____ .
c   Esta é (*your daughter*) _____ .
d   Estes são (*our sons*) _____ .
e   Aquele é (*my father*) _____ .

2   How would you say the following?

a   Ana is the youngest daughter.
b   Miguel is our tallest brother.
c   They are my older sons.
d   António is shorter.
e   Maria and Paula are taller.

▶ Leitura *Reading*

Listen to senhor Moura describing his family, then read the passage a couple of times to make sure you have understood it.

Tenho uma família bastante pequena. A minha mulher chama-se Rosa e é professora. Trabalha numa escola secundária em Braga. Ela é muito simpática e elegante. Temos três filhos: a Sônia, que é a mais velha, e a Catarina, a irmã, e o Roberto, o filho mais novo. A Sônia trabalha num hospital, e os outros dois são estudantes. O Roberto é alto e desportivo, e a Catarina é muito calma.

tenho	*I have*
bastante	*quite*
pequena	*small*
escola secundária	*secondary / high school*
muito	*very*
simpática	*nice*
elegante	*elegant*
temos	*we have*
os outros	*the other(s)*
desportivo	*sporty*
calma	*calm, easy-going*

Exercise

▶ 3 **Actividade três:** Now answer these questions about the família Moura.

a Como se chama a esposa do (*of*) senhor Moura?
b Onde é que ela trabalha?
c Quem é o filho mais novo?
d Como é a Catarina? (*What is she like?*)
e O que faz a Sônia?
f O Roberto é baixo?

Grammar

1 Ter *To have*

This is an important verb for you to learn, as you will be using it again later in the book. The main parts you need to know are:

ter	*to have*
tenho	I have
tens	you have (informal)
tem	you (singular) have, he / she / it has
temos	we have
têm	you (pl) have, they have

2 Describing people

Senhor Moura described his family, using adjectives to tell you about their characteristics. He used the words **simpático** (*nice*), **elegante** (*elegant*), **desportivo** (*sporty*), and **calmo** (*calm*). There are many words you can use to describe people. Here are a few more suggestions: remember to make the words agree with the person you are describing, by changing final **-o**, to **-a** (masc. →fem).

arrogante	*arrogant*
tímido	*shy*
sério/a	*serious*
engraçado	*funny*
preguiçoso/a	*lazy*
barulhento/a	*noisy*
orgulhoso/a	*proud*
alegre	*cheerful*
artístico/a	*artistic*
honesto/a	*honest*

3 *Ser* or *estar*: two verbs for 'to be'

Do you remember, in Units 1 and 2, the two ways of expressing *I am*, etc. in Portuguese? One is using the verb **ser** (for more permanent characteristics) and the other with the verb **estar** (when situations are more temporary). In the **Reading** passage, senhor Moura described the characteristics of his family members using **ser**, but if he had wanted to say how someone was at the moment, he would have used **estar**. To see how this works compare these two phrases:

Ela é calma. *She is calm*
  (i.e. a calm person, always).

Ela está calma. *She's calm* (at the moment).

It's important to think carefully before you use these verbs, but you'll get lots of practice as you progress through this course. Let's just check you know the parts of the two:

ser		estar	
sou	I am	estou	I am
és	you are (informal)	estás	you are (informal)
é	you are, he / she / it is	está	you are, he / she / it
somos	we are	estamos	we are
são	you (pl) are, they are	estão	you (pl) are, they are

Exercises

4 How would you say the following in Portuguese?

  a   Do you (sing) have a daughter?
  b   We have two children.
  c   Does she have a brother?
  d   I have a sister.
  e   Do you (pl) have children?

5 Find eight words in the wordsearch, which describe people's characteristics. The words may run up, down, diagonally, backwards or forwards.

P	R	E	G	U	I	Ç	O	S	O
A	T	C	L	I	A	T	I	T	V
T	S	A	O	S	S	E	N	A	I
R	E	L	I	E	P	E	E	V	T
I	N	M	N	Q	H	C	R	I	R
T	A	O	X	L	A	M	V	C	O
N	H	U	U	S	B	L	O	O	P
E	M	R	O	I	R	E	S	A	S
R	A	R	T	A	S	T	O	L	E
B	E	L	E	G	A	N	T	E	D

Documento

What type of person is this shop looking to employ?

▶ Diálogo 2

Senhor Moura is being asked about the ages of his children.

Tânia	Senhor Moura, quantos anos tem o seu filho mais novo?
Sr Moura	O mais novo, o Roberto, tem quinze anos.
Tânia	E as suas filhas?
Sr Moura	Pois, a Catarina tem dezassete anos e a Sónia vinte.
Tânia	E o senhor? Quantos anos tem?
Sr Moura	Eu? Ora bem, eu tenho . . . !

quantos anos tem?	*how old is he / she? / how old are you?*
anos	*years*
Ora bem	*well now!*

i Talking about age, how old somebody is, in Portuguese is done in terms of saying how many years someone has. **Tenho X anos** is how you would say *I am X (years old)*. Having a birthday, is known as **Fazer anos: Quando faz anos?** *When is your birthday? (Lit. when do you make years?)* If you want to congratulate someone on their birthday, say **Parabéns!** *Congratulations!* If you are lucky enough to be invited to a family birthday (or other) celebration, be prepared for a wonderful feast!

Exercises

6 There are two sentences muddled up here. Can you unscramble them?

   tem filha tem Quantos sua ? onze a anos Ela anos

▶ 7 Listen to the recorded activity on the CD.

Self-evaluation

You should now be able to do the following:

a Say this is my husband / wife.
b Say that is my brother / sister.
c Say this is our son / daughter.
d Say that is my youngest sister.
e Describe your husband / wife / teacher.
f Describe your own temperament.
g Ask someone how old they are.
h Say how old you are (you can be up to 20 at this stage!)

05

gostos pessoais

personal tastes

In this unit you will learn
- how to say what you like / dislike
- how to say what you prefer
- how to ask other people about their preferences

Before you begin

In this unit you will begin to find a mixture of forms of address (how to call someone 'you'). Remember that, between friends and young people, the **tu** form is used, and with older people, and people who do not know each other very well, you'll hear the polite forms of **o senhor/a senhora**, or **o/a** plus the person's name. Don't forget that the verb will often be used on its own, without a corresponding word for *'you'*. When talking to more than one person, you can either use the plurals **os senhores / as senhoras** or simply the plural form of the appropriate verb. You will see this demonstrated in the first dialogue. **Os senhores** can be used either to a group of men, or a mixed group or couple.

▶ Diálogo 1

Fátima is finding out if the Green family likes Portuguese food.

Fátima   Então, os senhores gostam da comida portuguesa?
Sr Green   Gostamos muito. A comida é saudável e muito deliciosa.
Fátima   Óptimo! A Senhora Green gosta de sardinhas?
Sra Green   Gosto, mas não muito. Têm muito sal. Gosto mais de frango.
Sr Green   Eu também gosto de frango. A nossa filha gosta muito de arroz de marisco.
Fátima   Não gostam do caldo verde? É tipicamente português.
Sra Green   Gostamos um pouco. E a Fátima, gosta da comida portuguesa?
Fátima   Claro, sou portuguesa, e os portugueses gostam imenso de comida!

os senhores gostam . . . ?	*do you (pl) like . . . ?*
a comida portuguesa	*Portuguese food*
gostamos	*we (do) like*
muito	*a lot, very*
saudável	*healthy*
delicioso/a	*delicious*
gosta . . . ?	*do you (he, she) like . . . ?*
as sardinhas	*sardines*
gosto	*I (do) like*
mas	*but*
têm	*they have*
(o) sal	*salt*
gosto mais	*I like more*
o frango	*chicken*

também	*also*
o arroz de marisco	*seafood rice*
não gostam . . . ?	*don't you like . . . ?*
o caldo verde	*shredded kale soup*
tipicamente	*typically*
um pouco	*a bit, a little*
claro	*of course*
gostam	*they like*
imenso	*a great deal, a lot*

Grammar

1 More on -*ar* verbs

Gostar, like some of the verbs you learnt in Units 2 and 3 (**morar, trabalhar, falar**), is what is known as a regular verb, i.e. it follows a normal pattern of endings for that group of verbs. It belongs to the biggest verb group in Portuguese – those which end in -**ar**. With only a few exceptions, all these verbs are formed in the same way:

* First you take off the -**ar** ending and you are left with what is called the stem.

    Gostar – ar = gost (the stem)

* Then you add on to this stem the appropriate ending according to whoever is doing the action.

* For -**ar** verbs, the endings you require are as follows:

    stem +
– o	*I*
– as	*you* (informal)
– a	*he, she, it, you* (polite)
– amos	*we*
– am	*they, you* (plural)

Here are a few examples:

fal<u>o</u>	*I speak*	gost<u>amos</u>	*we like*
mor<u>as</u>	*you live*	mor<u>am</u>	*they, you live*
trabalh<u>a</u>	*he / she works / you work*		

The meanings are sometimes ambiguous, so to make sure you really know who is doing the action, you may need to use the words for *he* (**ele**), *she* (**ela**), or *they* (**eles, elas**).

2 Gostar (de) *To like*

The verb **gostar** is followed by the word **de**, when that precedes a noun (thing) or a verb.

Gosta <u>de</u> frango?	*Do you like chicken?*
Sim, gosto.	*Yes, I do (like it).*
Gosto de comer frango.	*I like to eat chicken.*

The word **de** (which really serves no function in the sentence – it's one of those 'oddments' mentioned earlier in the book), combines with the words **o/a/os/as**, to form **do, da, dos, das**.

Gosto d<u>o</u> frango.	*I like **the** chicken.*
Gostamos d<u>as</u> sardinhas.	*We like **the** sardines.*
Ela não gosta d<u>a</u> comida.	*She doesn't like **the** food.*

3 A lot, a little

You can describe just how much you do or do not like something by using words such as **muito** (*a lot, much*), **um pouco** (*a little bit*), **não muito** (*not much*), and **imenso** (*a great deal*). This last one is used a lot by Portuguese people.

Exercises

1 How would you say the following?

   a Do Mr and Mrs Brito like chicken?
   b Don't you (**tu**) like the shredded kale soup?
   c No, I don't (like).
   d We like sardines a lot.
   e Paula likes seafood rice a little.
   f They like Portuguese food a great deal.

2 Choose the correct endings for the verbs in the sentences below. Here are the endings: **-o/-as/-a/-amos/-am**.

   a A Maria trabalh_____ num hospital.
   b Eu (I) não gost_____ do frango.
   c Nós (we) mor_____ em Lisboa.
   d Tu não gost_____ do caldo verde?
   e Os senhores Trindade fal_____ inglês.

3 Match up the questions on the left to the most likely answers on the right. Remember some verb forms can refer to different people.

a	Tu gostas do arroz de marisco?	i	Gostamos um pouco.
b	Os senhores gostam da comida?	ii	O Miguel gosta muito.
c	A Paula não gosta do frango?	iii	Sim, gosto muito.
d	Quem (*who*) gosta das sardinhas?	iv	Não, não gosta.
e	O seu filho não gosta do caldo verde?	v	Não, ela não gosta muito.

Documento 1

What is this restaurant ad inviting you to come and try?

▶ Leitura *Reading*

Listen to the passage and read it carefully. Nuno talks about his family's preferences for different countries. See if you can work out some of the reasons for their likes and dislikes.

Bom, gostamos todos da Suíça, porque é um país muito limpo, mas é um pouco caro para nós. Pessoalmente, prefiro a Austrália, porque tem um clima agradável. A minha mulher prefere a Dinamarca, porque ela gosta imenso da comida dinamarquesa. Não gostamos muito do Japão porque é muito movimentado. Preferimos um lugar mais calmo, como a Holanda. Os nossos filhos preferem o barulho. Eles gostam imenso dos Estados Unidos.

a Suíça	*Switzerland*
porque	*because*
um país	*a country*
limpo	*clean*
caro	*expensive*
para nós	*for us*
pessoalmente	*personally*
prefiro	*I prefer*
um clima	*climate*
agradável	*agreeable, enjoyable*
prefere	*she / he prefers / you prefer*
a Dinamarca	*Denmark*
a comida dinamarquesa	*Danish food*
o Japão	*Japan*
movimentado	*busy, crowded*
preferimos	*we prefer*
um lugar	*a place*
calmo	*calm*
a Holanda	*Holland*
preferem	*they / you prefer*
o barulho	*noise*

Exercise

▶ 4 **Actividade quatro:** Without looking back at the **Reading** passage, see if you can answer these questions.

a A família do Nuno gosta da Suíça?
b Porquê? (*Why?*)
c Porque é que o Nuno prefere a Austrália?

d Eles gostam do Japão?
e Quem prefere a Dinamarca?
f Porque é que os filhos preferem os Estados Unidos?

Grammar

4 Describing places

In Unit 4 you learnt some words (adjectives) for describing people. In the reading passage you were introduced to some words to use when describing places (towns, countries), such as **limpo**, **caro**, and **movimentado**.

You might also want to try out the following:

barulhento/a	*noisy*
sujo/a	*dirty*
aborrecido/a	*boring*
desagradável	*unpleasant*
moderno/a	*modern*
antigo / velho/a	*old*
barato/a	*cheap*
bonito/a	*nice, pretty (picturesque)*
histórico/a	*historical*
interessante	*interesting*
cultural	*cultural*

5 (O) que prefere? *What do you prefer?*

When asking people about their preferences about various items, you can ask them (**o**) **que prefere?**:

O que prefere – frango
ou sardinhas?
What do you prefer? Chicken or sardines?

You can also use **qual prefere?** (*Which do you prefer?*):

Qual prefere – o Japão
ou a Holanda?
Which do you prefer? Japan or Holland?

Don't forget to make the verb plural (**preferem**) if you are talking to more than one person.

Que preferem – vinho
ou cerveja?
What do you prefer? Wine or beer?

Documento 2

What kind of holidays (**férias**) is this advertisement inviting you to take this year?

ESTE ANO
faça férias
diferentes!

Exercises

5 Try out the following phrases using what you have just learnt.

a Say you prefer England because it's historical.
b Ask which Sr Antunes prefers – Switzerland or Denmark.
c Say that Sônia prefers Italy because it's interesting.
d Ask which Mr and Mrs Oliveira prefer – America or Japan.
e Say that we prefer Holland because it's pretty.

▶ 6 Listen to the activity on your CD to practise talking about what food and drink you like.

7 Fill in the puzzle with words used to describe various places. The first word is put in for you.

Self-evaluation

Now see what you have learnt in this unit. Can you:

a ask someone (singular, polite) if they like chicken?
b say that you like sardines, a little?
c say that Miguel likes Portuguese food a great deal?
d ask Sr Green if he doesn't like the shredded kale soup?
e say that you prefer Portugal because it's interesting?
f ask Mr and Mrs Oliveira which they prefer: Italy or Japan?
g say that we prefer Danish food?

06

em casa
at home

In this unit you will learn
- how to describe your house
- how to say where things are
- how to say 'there is' / 'there are'

Can you remember how *in* and *on*, and *in a* and *on a* are said in Portuguese? Have a quick look back at Unit 3 to check that you are completely familiar with forms of these expressions before learning new ground in this unit.

Before you begin

The word **casa** basically means *house* in Portuguese, although it encompasses the overall general idea of a residence. For example, you may hear Portuguese people speaking about their **casa**, when, in fact, they live in an apartment. In most cities in Portugal, you will find people living in some kind of apartment: some of them are ultra-modern, while others are very traditional flats in old buildings. In the smaller towns, and in the countryside, you will find more houses. **Em casa** means *at home* and the expressions **vou a casa**, and **vou para casa**, both mean *I'm going/I go* (vou) *home*.

▶ Leitura *Reading*

Roberto is talking about where he lives. Listen to the recording and then read the passage. How much of it can you understand without looking at the vocabulary list?

Moro em Lisboa, num apartamento moderno. Fica no quinto andar dum edifício muito alto. O apartamento não é muito grande. Há dois quartos, uma sala, uma cozinha e uma casa de banho. Gosto muito do apartamento porque é fácil de limpar. O edifício tem elevador mas, de vez em quando, não funciona. Esta é a única coisa de que não gosto!

um edifício	*building*
grande	*big*
há	*there are*
o quarto	*bedroom*
uma sala	*a living room, lounge*
uma cozinha	*a kitchen*
uma casa de banho	*a bathroom*
é fácil de limpar	*it's easy to clean*
(o) elevador	*lift*
de vez em quando	*from time to time, sometimes*
não funciona	*it doesn't work*
a única coisa	*the only thing*
que	*that, which*

So, how did you get on? Did you manage to guess some of the names of rooms? Many Portuguese words are fairly similar to English ones, and if you stretch your imagination a little bit, you can often come up with the correct words. For example, **quarto** is similar to the English 'quarters' (as in 'living quarters'), **sala** is like 'salon' and **cozinha** like 'cuisine'.

▶ Diálogo 1

Now listen to Ana Maria talking to a friend about her house in the country town of Elvas.

Ana Maria   Gosto imenso da minha casa.
Júlia   Como é a casa?
Ana Maria   Bem, é bastante grande, e tem dois andares. Fica no Bairro de Boa Vista, e é típica da região.
Júlia   Quantas assoalhadas tem?
Ana Maria   Em baixo há uma sala de estar, e uma de jantar, e também uma cozinha grande.
Júlia   E em cima?
Ana Maria   Em cima há dois quartos pequenos e um quarto grande com terraço e uma casa de banho bonita.

Como é a casa?	*What's the house like?*
(o) Bairro de Boa Vista	*Boa Vista district, area*
típica da região	*typical of the region*
quantas assoalhadas tem?	*how many rooms does it have?*
em baixo	*downstairs*
uma sala de estar	*living room*
uma sala de jantar	*dining room*
em cima	*upstairs*
com terraço	*with a balcony*

Exercise

1 Look at the two house plans below. One of them is Roberto's apartment, and the other is the downstairs of Ana Maria's house. Which is which?

(a)

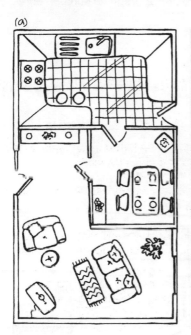

(b)

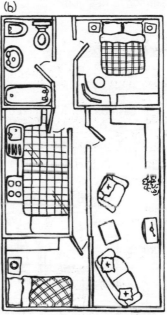

Grammar

1 Há *There is, there are*

This little word is extremely versatile as you can use it to talk about both singular, or plural, objects:

Há uma sala.	*There is a lounge.*
Há dois quartos.	*There are two bedrooms.*

It can be used as a question: *is there, are there?*

Há uma cozinha?   *Is there a kitchen?*

and is turned into the negative *there is not, there are not,* by placing the word **não** before it:

Não há uma casa de banho.   *There isn't a bathroom.*

i In many Portuguese buildings, you will need to use the lift. It is vital, then, to understand the symbols for the different floors. The ground floor is called **o rés-do-chão**, and in the lift you will see it abbreviated to **r/c**. All the other floors are simply numbered 1°, 2°, 3°, and so on. The ° is the last letter of the appropriate number: primeir<u>o</u>, segund<u>o</u>, and so on.

Exercises

2   Look at the following house plan, and complete the dialogue below, to describe the house.

A casa da família Ferreira é antiga e ___ da região. Na casa há ___ quartos. Há dois ___ e um ___ com ___ . Em cima também ___ uma ___ ___ ___ . Em ___ há uma ___, uma sala ___ estar e uma ___ ___ ___ .

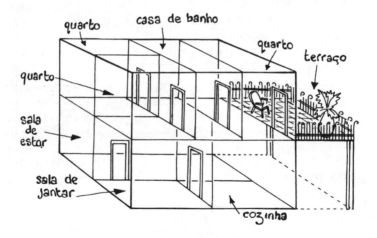

3   Can you talk about your own house? Start with . . . **a minha casa** . . . , and choose words from each box to help you with the description. If you need some help, there's a typical answer in the **Key to the exercises**.

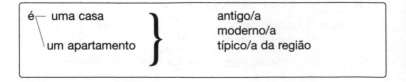

```
fica ┌─num edifício ┐                      rés-do-chão
     └─num bairro   ┘ antigo, moderno   no primeiro
                                           segundo  ┐ andar
                                           terceiro ┘
```

```
                em cima           em baixo
na casa há ┌─1,2,3 quartos      uma cozinha
           ├─uma casa de banho  uma sala de jantar
           └─um terraço         uma sala de estar
```

Gosto / Não gosto da minha casa.

▶ Leitura *Reading*

Listen carefully to a 'through the keyhole' guide to Paula's house, as she describes where various pieces of furniture are located. Then read the passage below again, to make sure you have understood as much as you can.

Primeiro, estamos na sala, onde há um sofá em frente da lareira, e ao lado do sofá, duas poltronas. Há um vaso de flores em cima da estante. Na cozinha há um fogão entre o frigorífico e a máquina de lavar. O meu gato está debaixo da mesa. No meu quarto há um quadro bonito na parede, e detrás da porta há um armário. Na casa de banho há um chuveiro.

primeiro	*first of all*
onde	*where*
um sofá	*a sofa*
em frente de	*in front of*
a lareira	*fireplace*
ao lado de	*next to*
a poltrona	*armchair*
um vaso de flores	*a vase of flowers*
em cima de	*on top of*
a estante	*bookcase*
um fogão	*a cooker*
entre	*in between*
o frigorífico	*fridge*

a máquina de lavar	washing machine
o gato	cat
debaixo de	underneath
a mesa	table
um quadro	a picture
na (= em + a)	on the
a parede	wall
detrás de	behind
a porta	door
um armário	wardrobe, cupboard
um chuveiro	a shower

Exercise

▶4 **Actividade quatro:** Can you answer these questions, based on the reading passage?

a Onde está o sofá?
b O que há (*what is there*) em cima da estante?
c Onde está o gato?
d Há uma mesa na cozinha?
e O que há no quarto da Paula?
f Há uma poltrona na casa de banho?

Grammar

2 How to say 'in', 'on', 'under'

The **Reading** passage introduced you to some of the more common Portuguese expressions for describing where things (or people) are. These words are known as prepositions: the word *position* should help you to remember their function. Many of the Portuguese prepositions are made up of more than one word, and often end with the word -**de**. Did you notice in the passage how the **de** combined, or contracted, with the words for *the* or *a*? You should now be becoming familiar with these contracted forms – they are very common in Portuguese. For example:

detrás **da** poltrona (= de + a) *behind the chair*
debaixo **duma** mesa (= de + uma) *under a table*

You will meet more of these as you go along.

Don't forget when describing the location of items which can move – use the verb **estar** for *is* (**está**) and *are* (**estão**).

Exercises

5   Look at the diagram of Jorge's **sala de estar,** and answer true (**verdadeiro**) or false (**falso**) to the following statements:

Na sala de estar:

a   Há três poltronas.
b   O gato está detrás da estante.
c   Há um vaso de flores debaixo da mesa.
d   Há um sofá em frente da lareira.
e   A estante está entre as poltronas.
f   Há uma poltrona ao lado da mesa.

6   How would you say the following?

a   The cat is on top of the fridge.
b   There is a cupboard next to the bookcase.
c   Is there a sofa behind the table?
d   The shower is not in the kitchen.
e   The cooker is next to the washing machine.
f   Is the cat in front of the armchair?

Documento

a   How many bedrooms are there in this advertised house?
b   Is there a fireplace in the living room?

CASA DE CAMPO
RIBATEJO

Linda moradia, sala c/ lareira, 3 quartos, 2 wc,
c/ quintal e garagem. Sossego e ar puro.
Tel. 793 54 40/88 – Sr. Ferreira

---

n.b. The abbreviation c/ means **com** (with).

▶ 7 Listen to this short description of a house by a local estate agent, and decide whether the following statements are True or False. You will hear the correct answers on the recording. There may be some new words, but you should be able to guess their meaning from the context.

1 Casa Rosa is an old house.   T/F
2 It has a kitchen-diner.   T/F
3 There are kitchen appliances included in the price. T/F
4 There are only two bedrooms.   T/F
5 The garage is big enough for two cars.   T/F

Self-evaluation

You should now be able to do the following:

a Say what kind of residence you have.
b Describe which rooms your house has.
c Ask someone what their house is like.
d Say you have a big / small kitchen / bathroom.
e Say that there are 2 / 3 / 4 / 5 bedrooms.
f Say that there isn't a living room / dining room.
g Say where your sofa is.
h Describe where the fridge is.
i Ask someone what there is in the bedroom.

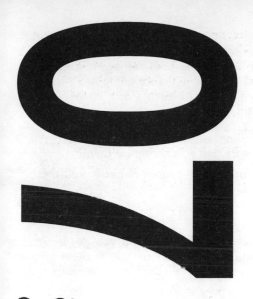

07

a vida diária

daily life

In this unit you will learn
- how to talk about daily activities
- the days of the week
- the times of the day
- numbers 21–100

Before you begin

In this unit you will be encountering the numbers from 21 to 100. You learnt from 0 to 20 in Unit 3, so perhaps it would be a good idea if you revised them now before going any further. There's nothing worse than trying to learn a new set of words when previous ones are still rather vague.

▶ Listen to your recording now, and you will hear ten numbers you have met before. Do you recognize them?

What about working the other way round? What would these numbers be in Portuguese?

12   6   18   2   15   10

If you are happy with these numbers, then on you go; if not, then spend a couple of minutes every day practising them until they are firmly planted in your mind – then you'll be ready for the next set.

▶ Leitura *Reading*

Rosa is describing her daily routine. Listen to and read the text, and see how many daily activities you can work out. Also listen out for what time she does them.

Levanto-me às sete horas da manhã. Tomo banho e visto-me. Às sete e meia tomo o pequeno almoço, e saio para apanhar o autocarro às oito horas. Chego ao escritório às oito e vinte, e começo o trabalho às oito e meia. Ao meio-dia almoço. Saio do trabalho às cinco e um quarto e chego a casa às seis horas da tarde. Janto por volta das sete, e às quartas-feiras à noite vou a uma aula de inglês. Deito-me às dez menos um quarto.

So, how did you get on? The activities Rosa mentions are:

▶		
levanto-me	*I get up*
tomo banho	*I have a bath*
visto-me	*I get dressed*
tomo o pequeno almoço	*I have breakfast*
saio para apanhar o autocarro	*I leave to catch the bus*
chego	*I arrive*
começo o trabalho	*I begin work*
almoço	*I have lunch*
janto	*I dine*
vou a uma aula de inglês	*I go to an English class*
deito-me	*I go to bed*

The times of her activities mentioned were:

▶	às sete horas da manhã	*at seven in the morning*
	às sete e meia	*at half past seven*
	às oito horas	*at eight o'clock*
	às oito e vinte	*at twenty past eight*
	às oito e meia	*at half past eight*
	ao meio-dia	*at noon, midday*
	às cinco e um quarto	*at quarter past five*
	às seis horas da tarde	*at six in the evening*
	por volta das sete	*around seven*
	às quartas-feiras à noite	*on Wednesday evenings*
	às dez menos um quarto	*at quarter to ten*

Grammar

1 Two irregular verbs

With the exception of **visto-me**, **saio**, and **vou**, all the verbs listed as Rosa's activities fall into the regular group of **-ar** verbs, the formation of which you learnt in Unit 5. Therefore, *she arrives* will be **chega**, *we begin* will be **começamos**, and *they dine* will be **jantam**. Have a quick look back at Unit 5, if you cannot remember the various verb endings. **Visto-me** will be dealt with later in this unit, but the two remaining verbs belong to groups which follow different patterns for many of their endings.

		sair *to go out*			**ir** *to go*	
I	(eu)	saio	*I go out*	(eu)	vou	*I go*
you	(tu)	sais	*you go out*	(tu)	vais	*you go*
he	(ele) ⎫			(ele) ⎫		
she	(ela) ⎬	sai	*he / she / you go(es) out*	(ela) ⎬	vai	*he / she / you go(es)*
you (polite)	⎭			⎭		
we	(nós)	saimos	*we go out*	(nós)	vamos	*we go*
they	(eles, elas) ⎫		*they / you go out*	(eles, elas) ⎫	vão	*they / you go*
you (pl)	⎭ saem			⎭		

2 Visto-me *I get dressed*

You will have noticed some of the verbs describing Rosa's activities had a **-me** joined on to them. Remember also, that you met this kind of verb in Unit 1, when giving your name (**chamo-me**). The **-me** actually means '*myself*', and so the literal meanings of these verbs are – *I get myself up*, *I call myself*, *I get myself dressed*, and so on. When you want to talk about other people doing these actions, there are different 'self' words. Here is the verb *to get up* with all the appropriate end-words.

(eu)	levanto-me	*I get up*
(tu)	levantas-te	*you get up*
(ele, ela)	levanta-se	*he / she / + you get(s) up*
(nós)	levantamo-nos	*we get up*
(eles, elas)	levantam-se	*they / + you get up*

Be careful with the *we* form because it loses the final -s from the verb ending.

3 As horas *Time*

The Portuguese talk about time in terms of hours (**as horas**)

A que horas . . . ?   *At what time . . . ?*

* Time on the hour is easily expressed as follows:

  às + the number of + horas + da manhã (in the morning)
  at   the hour   (o'clock) da tarde (in the afternoon, evening)
                                    da noite (at night)

  às   sete   (horas)   da   manhã   7 a.m.
  às   nove   (horas)   da   noite   9 p.m.

  After the number, the word **horas** is optional.

* Time past the hour is expressed thus:

  às   +   the hour   + e (*and*) um quarto (*a quarter*)
                              meia (*half*)
                              . . . minutos (*minutes*)

  às cinco e vinte   5.20
  às três e um quarto   3.15
  às oito e meia   8.30

  Again, you may want to specify whether you mean morning, afternoon or evening.

* Time to the hour is expressed in a couple of ways. Here is one of them.

às	+	next full hour	+	menos	+	minutes/um quarto
				(less)		
às dez menos vinte				9.40		

Note:

ao meio-dia	*at midday*
à meia-noite	*at midnight*
à uma hora	*at one o'clock*

▶ Listen to some times on the recording and try to work out what they are.

▶ 4 Os números 21–100 *Numbers 21–100*

To deal more effectively with time, you need numbers up to 60 at least, and as numbers are a part of our everyday lives, here is the next set for you to start learning.

21	vinte e um/uma	50	cinquenta
22	vinte e dois/duas	60	sessenta
23	vinte e três	70	setenta
24	vinte e quatro	80	oitenta
25	vinte e cinco	90	noventa
30	trinta	100	cem (cento)
40	quarenta		

Can you see the pattern of formation? You simply use the word **e** (*and*) to join the two lots of digits together. Don't forget, wherever one, or two occur, you must decide to use either the masculine or feminine form. e.g. vinte e duas mesas, 22 tables. There are two forms for 100: **cem** is used for a round one hundred, and **cento** for any combination over a hundred (101, 125, and so on).

Listen to the numbers on your recording, and try to repeat each one in the pause.

▶ Now let's have a quick practice with some of these new numbers. Listen and say what you think each number is.

Exercises

1 Look at Maurício's diary entry for Wednesday (**quarta-feira**), and complete the five statements about his daily activities.

Quarta-feira			
7.15 a.m.	levanto-me	5.20 p.m.	saio do
8.30 a.m.	saio		trabalho
9.00 a.m.	começo o	6.45 p.m.	janto
	trabalho	7.40 p.m.	aula de japonês
1.00 p.m.	almoço	11.25 p.m.	deito-me

a   O Maurício _____ às 7.15.
b   Começa o trabalho às _____ .
c   Ele _____ às ___ menos _____ _____ .
d   Às 7.40 tem uma _____ _____ _____ .
e   O Maurício almoça _____ _____ .

2 The numbers below represent the house numbers on the doors. Can you match them up correctly?

a vinte e sete   **b** setenta e sete   **c** noventa e três
d trinta e cinco   **e** quarenta e um   **f** noventa e seis

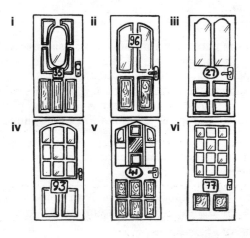

3 Match the clock times to the statements about the daily activities that various people do.

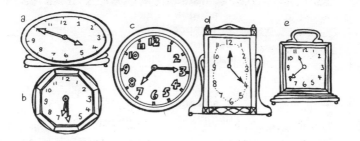

i   A Maria levanta-se às seis e meia.
ii   O Jorge almoça ao meio-dia e vinte.
iii O Manuel sai do trabalho às cinco menos dez.
iv   A Lídia janta às sete e um quarto.
v   O Filipe chega ao trabalho às onze menos vinte.

4 Can you answer the following questions about your own daily routines? There are some sample answers for you to check in the **Key to the exercises** at the back of the book.

a   What time do you get up?
b   What time do you have lunch?
c   What time do you arrive home?
d   What time do you go to bed?

▶ Diálogo 1

Rui and João are talking about their weekend routines.

Rui   A que horas se levanta aos sábados?
João Geralmente às oito e meia. Eu e a minha mulher vamos às compras, e o nosso filho vai jogar futebol com os amigos.
Rui   E a que horas almoçam?
João Em geral não comemos muito ao almoço. Jantamos por volta das sete horas. E o Rui?
Rui   Na minha casa também jantamos mais tarde, e depois saímos para passear na praça.
João O que faz aos domingos?
Rui   Bem, a minha mulher levanta-se e come cedo, e parte para a igreja. Passamos o resto do dia em família, e não nos deitamos muito tarde.

aos sábados	on Saturdays
geralmente/em geral	generally
às compras	shopping
amigos	friends
vai jogar futebol	goes to play football
comemos	we eat
mais tarde	later
depois	then, after
para passear	(in order) to stroll around
a praça	town square
aos domingos	on Sundays
come	she eats
cedo	early
parte	departs, leaves
a igreja	church
passamos	we spend
o resto do dia	the rest of the day
em família	together, as a family

Grammar

▶ 1 Os dias da semana *The days of the week*

segunda-feira	Monday	**sexta-feira**	Friday
terça-feira	Tuesday	**sábado**	Saturday
quarta-feira	Wednesday	**domingo**	Sunday
quinta-feira	Thursday		

The days of the week are 'numbered' – 2nd, 3rd, etc. They are all feminine words. The weekend days are masculine. In spoken Portuguese, it is usual to drop the word '**feira**', and speak in terms of **terça**, **quinta**, etc.

na segunda	*on Monday*
no domingo	*on Sunday*
às sextas-feiras	*on Fridays*
aos sábados	*on Saturdays*

Sometimes the days are written with a capital letter, but there is no consistency.

2 A que horas se levanta? *What time do you get up?*

You may have noticed the changed position of the 'self' word, se, in this question. In Rosa's earlier description she said **levanto-me**. Whenever you have one of these verbs, known as reflexives, the reflexive bit of it (the 'self' word) is placed before the verb if a question is being asked.

3 Não nos deitamos tarde *We don't go to bed late*

This is another example where the reflexives change their position and go in front of the verb – wherever a negative is used. So you could have:

Levanta-se cedo.   *He gets up early.*

but

Não se levanta tarde.   *He doesn't get up late.*

4 *-er* and *-ir* verb types

Up to now you have worked with -ar type verbs, and a few irregular verbs. There are two other main verb groups, examples of which you saw in the dialogue. They are -er and -ir groups.

comer *to eat*		**partir** *to depart/leave*	
eu	como	eu	parto
tu	comes	tu	partes
ele, ela, *you*	come	ele, ela, *you*	parte
nós	comemos	nós	partimos
eles, elas,		eles, elas,	
you (pl)	comem	*you* (pl)	partem

Can you see the similarities between the two? Earlier, you had the verb **visto-me** (*I get dressed*). This belongs to the -ir group (**vestir**), but the *I* person is slightly different.

5 How to say 'to', 'to the'

Like previous contracted forms, the preposition **a** (*to, at*) combines with the words for *the*, to form the following:

ao = a + o	aos = a + os	à = a + a	às = a + as
ao trabalho	*to work*	à igreja	*to (the) church*
aos escritórios	*to the offices*	às casas	*to the houses*

Documento

When can you **not** visit this establishment?

cervejaria
XANA

PETISCOS

CARACÓIS

PÃO COM CHOURIÇO

Aberto das 7:30 às 22:00h.
Encerra à 4° feira, de manhã.

**Bairro da Malagueira
Rua da Conduta, 16
Tel. 735862**

Exercises

5 How would you say the following?

a I get up early.
b He does not go to bed late.
c What time do you (pl) get dressed?
d We do not get dressed quickly (**rapidamente**).
e What are they called?
f What time do you (informal) get up?

6 The following people have lost their verbs. Choose the correct form of the appropriate verb from the list underneath. The infinitive of the verb you want is in brackets at the start of each sentence.

a (**compreender**) Ele ___ (*understands*)
b (**partir**) A senhora ___ (*departs*)
c (**comer**) Nós ___ (*eat*)
d (**viver**) Os senhores Neto ___ (*live*)
e (**abrir**) Tu ___ (*open*)
f (**beber**) O senhor Smith ___ (*drinks*)

parte	come	vivem	compreende
abres	bebe	partes	vivemos
compreendo	comemos	abro	bebemos

▶ Diálogo 2

Senhor Buisel has to get to the airport on time. He asks his neighbour what time it is.

Sr Buisel	Bom dia, Dona Ana Maria.
Da Ana Maria	Bom dia, senhor Buisel.
Sr Buisel	Desculpe, mas a senhora sabe que horas são?
Da Ana Maria	São duas menos cinco.
Sr Buisel	Obrigado. Preciso de ir ao aeroporto. Até breve.

Sabe que horas são?	*Do you know what time it is?*
preciso de	*I need*
o aeroporto	*airport*
até breve	*see you soon*

Grammar

Que horas são? *What time is it?*

As with the time of day, earlier in this unit, asking and telling the time uses the word **horas**, and literally asks *what hours are they?* The answer follows the same form: **são x horas** (or **é**, with *one o'clock*, *midday* and *midnight*). All the other times *to* and *from* the hour are the same as those you learnt earlier.

São três horas.	*It's 3 o'clock.*
São cinco menos vinte.	*It's twenty to five.*
É meia-noite e um quarto.	*It's quarter past midnight.*

▶ Listen to some more time phrases on the recording.

i Senhor Buisel called his neighbour Dona Ana Maria. The word Dona is used as a sign of respect when talking to older ladies, whether they are married or not. You may also hear **a senhora Dona Ana Maria**. Both of these forms of address can be used with verbs to convey the polite form of *you*.

A Dona Patrícia está boa?	*Are you well (Dona Patrícia)?*

Portuguese forms of address are extremely varied, as you keep finding out. Remember to take your cues from the people around you, and, when in doubt, err on the over-polite side.

Self-evaluation

You should now be able to:

a   Describe your daily routine.
b   Ask someone what time they get up.
c   Count to 100 out loud.
d   Say that we do not go to bed until (**até**) 10.30 p.m.
e   Ask Paulo what time he has lunch on Sundays.
f   Say that you do not eat much on Tuesdays.
g   Ask Jorge what time he goes to church.
h   Ask someone what time it is.

08

free time

o tempo livre

In this unit you will learn
- what a Brazilian Portuguese speaker sounds like
- how to talk about activities you enjoy
- how to ask people what they like doing in their free time
- four very irregular verbs: *listen*, *read*, *see* and *do*

Before you begin

Before tackling the new verbs you are going to meet in this unit, it might be a good idea to look back at the explanations about the basic verb types: Unit 5 for -ar verbs and Unit 7 for -er and -ir verbs.

▶ Diálogo 1

Some market research is being carried out in the street to find out what people like doing in their free time. Listen to the conversation and then read it over. The interviewer is talking to a group of three passers-by.

Entrevistador	Boa tarde. Com licença, posso fazer uma pergunta?
Laura	Claro. O que quer saber?
Entrevistador	O que é que vocês gostam de fazer no tempo livre?
Laura	Ora bem. No meu tempo livre gosto de ouvir música clássica, e de pintar.
José	Eu gosto de ir à piscina, ou de vez em quando gosto de passear no campo.
Entrevistador	E você? O que gosta de fazer no seu tempo de lazer?
Ana	Pois, gosto muito de ler, e de ver televisão.
Entrevistador	E o que gosta de ver?
Ana	Adoro as telenovelas brasileiras.
Entrevistador	Óptimo!

posso . . . ?	*may I . . . ?*
fazer uma pergunta	*to ask a question*
claro	*of course*
o que quer saber?	*what do you want to know?*
o que é que vocês gostam de fazer?	*what do you (pl) like to do?*
no tempo livre	*in your free time*
no seu tempo de lazer	*in your free/leisure time*
ora bem	*well*
ouvir	*to listen to*
música clássica	*classical music*
pintar	*to paint*
a piscina	*swimming pool*
o campo	*countryside*

e você?	*and you?*
o que gosta de fazer?	*what do you like doing?*
ler	*to read*
ver	*to watch (see)*
a televisão	*television*
as telenovelas brasileiras	*Brazilian soap operas*

Grammar

1 Você, vocês *You*

Did you notice that the interviewer spoke with a different accent? That's because he was Brazilian. He also used a different form of address from the ones you have already met. **Você**, and the plural **vocês**, is the most common way to say *you* in Brazil. The corresponding verb forms are the same as the singular and plural polite *you* in continental Portugal. You will also hear these forms of address in Portugal, but they are less formal than the ones you have so far learnt.

2 Posso? *May / can I?*

The usual response if someone asks **posso?** is **pode** (*you can*) or **sim pode** (*yes you can*) or even **claro que pode** (*of course you can*). Other forms of this verb you may need are:

tu podes
ele / ela / você (+ other 'you' forms) pode
nós podemos
eles / elas / vocês podem

Posso? is what you would say if you wanted to take a spare chair from someone's table in a restaurant or café.

3 O que (é que) gosta de fazer? *What do you like to do (doing)?*

You should remember that in Unit 5, the verb **gostar de** (*to like*) was used with various nouns (things) to describe what you do or don't like. Now you can use the same verb to talk about things you like doing, and as **gostar** is a straightforward **-ar** verb, you can also talk about other people's likes without too many problems.

| O Nuno gosta de pintar. | *Nuno likes painting (to paint).* |
| Gostamos de ouvir música. | *We like listening to music.* |

In addition to some of the activities listed in the dialogue, here are some more suggestions for things you may do in your free time.

praticar desportos	*playing sports*
ir ao teatro	*going to the theatre*
nadar	*swimming*
andar	*walking*
viajar	*travelling*
costurar	*sewing / making clothes*
trabalhar no jardim / jardinar	*working in the garden*
dançar	*dancing*
fazer bricolage	*doing 'do-it-yourself'*
fazer colecção de	*collecting . . .*

Exercises

1 See if you can do the following:

a Ask Maria what she likes doing in her free time.
b Say that you like sewing.
c Ask the da Silvas if they like travelling.
d Ask José and Nuno if they like playing sports.
e Say what you don't like doing.
f Ask someone you know very well if they like swimming in their free time.

▶ 2 **Actividade dois:** You are walking through Oporto when you are stopped in the street by an interviewer who wants to find out what you and your family enjoy doing in your free time. As you are the only one who can speak Portuguese, you will have to speak for your family. Follow the prompts and complete the conversation.

Entrevistadora	Bom dia. Com licença, posso fazer umas perguntas?
a **You**	*Say yes, of course you can.*
Entrevistadora	São portugueses?
b **You**	*No, you're not Portuguese. You're all English. Tell him what city you're from.*
Entrevistadora	Mas fala português?
c **You**	*Say yes, you speak some Portuguese.*

Entrevistadora	Muito bem. Então, o que é que gosta de fazer no tempo livre?
d You	*Say that you like going to the theatre.*
Entrevistadora	E a sua família?
e You	*Say that your husband / wife likes to work in the garden, and that your children like playing sports.*
Entrevistadora	E vocês gostam de visitar Portugal?
f You	*Say, of course!*

Documento 1

Would you be interested in this establishment if you liked artistic pursuits?

> ### Casa do Brasil
> CENTRO DE LÍNGUA, ARTE E CULTURA

▶ Monólogo 1

Listen to and read Sônia's account of the activities she enjoys doing, and how often she does them.

> Gosto muito de ouvir música. Às vezes ouço a música rock mas geralmente prefiro a música jazz. Aos fins de semana passo muito tempo a ler. Leio revistas e jornais, e gosto de livros românticos. Vou muitas vezes à biblioteca para ler.

às vezes	*sometimes*
ouço	*I listen to*
aos fins de semana	*at the weekend(s)*
passo tempo a ler	*I spend time reading*
leio	*I read*
revistas e jornais	*magazines and newspapers*
livros românticos	*romantic books*
muitas vezes	*often, many times*
a biblioteca	*library*

▶ Monólogo 2

Now find out what Nuno gets up to, and when.

> Gosto imenso de praticar desportos. Adoro jogar ténis, e todos os dias tento jogar pelo menos uma hora. Também gosto de navegar na Internet, e todas as noites vejo a televisão. O meu programa preferido é 'Quem quer ser milionário'?

jogar ténis	to play tennis
todos os dias	each, every day
tento	I try
pelo menos	at least
navegar na Internet	to surf the web (Internet)
todas as noites	every night
vejo	I watch, see
o meu programa preferido	my favourite programme
Quem quer ser milionário?	Who wants to be a Millionaire?

Grammar

1 Sometimes, often, never

There are many words to describe how frequently people do activities; some appeared in the monologues (**às vezes, muitas vezes, todos os dias, todas as noites**). Here are some further suggestions:

nunca	never
de vez em quando	sometimes
uma vez por (semana)	once a (week)
cada (mês)	each (month)
todos os anos	every year
poucas vezes	few times, a little

In general, these expressions go before the verb,

Nunca vou ao cinema.   I *never go to the cinema.*

although some will fit naturally at the end of a sentence.

Vejo a televisão todos os dias. I *watch television every day.*

2 Ouço, leio, vejo, faço I *listen, read, see, do (make)*

The verbs **ouvir, ler, ver,** and **fazer** are all irregular in some way or other. Here are the four verbs in full:

	ouvir *to listen*		**ler** *to read*	
(eu)	ouço	*I listen*	leio	*I read*
(tu)	ouves	*you listen*	lês	*you read*
(ele, ela, você, o senhor)	ouve	*he / she / you listen(s)*	lê	*he / she / you read(s)*
(nós)	ouvimos	*we listen*	lemos	*we read*
(eles, elas, vocês, os senhores)	ouvem	*they / you listen*	lêem	*they / you read*
	ver *to watch, see*		**fazer** *to do/make*	
(eu)	vejo	*I watch, see*	faço	*I do, make*
(tu)	vês	*you watch, see*	fazes	*you do, make*
(ele, ela, você o senhor)	vê	*he / she / you watch(es), see(s)*	faz	*he / she / you do(es) make(s)*
(nós)	vemos	*we watch, see*	fazemos	*we do, make*
(eles, elas, vocês, os senhores)	vêem	*they / you watch, see*	fazem	*they / you do, make*

3 Para *In order to*

Sónia said she goes to the library **para ler** (*to read*), and you may have wondered why you needed the word **para**, when in fact **ler** already means *to read*. This also arose in the last unit, when Rosa said she leaves her house **para apanhar o autocarro** *to catch the bus*. In fact you need to use the word **para** (*in order to*) before any verb, when it is your intention or objective to do something.

Vou à cidade para fazer as compras.   *I go / am going to town (in order) to do the shopping.*

Exercises

3   Fill in the gaps in the monologue below, choosing from the words in the box that follows.

Eu gosto de ler ___ de aventura. ___ todos os ___ , e também ___ a televisão. O meu marido ___ música clássica, e ___ golfe. Ele ___ ___ o jornal, mas ___ de ler revistas. As minhas filhas ___ à discoteca ___ as semanas, e de ___ em ___ ___ colecção de bonecas (*dolls*).

ouve	nunca	gosta	leio
vão	livros	joga	dias
lê	vejo	todas	vez
quando	fazem		

4   Link up the statements on the left with the verbs on the right, using **para** (*in order to*) to make complete sentences.

   a   Vou à biblioteca   i   fazer as compras.
   b   Paula vai ao escritório   ii   dançar.
   c   Vamos ao centro desportivo   iii ler os livros.
   d   Ela vai ao supermercado   iv   jogar ténis.
   e   Eles vão à piscina   v   nadar.
   f   Mónica vai à discoteca   vi   trabalhar.

5   Fill in the crossword puzzle with expressions of frequency. The first has been done for you.

Documento 2

How often is this restaurant open?

RESTAURANTE - BAR

2 IRMÃOS

ABERTO TODOS OS DIAS

Especialidades da Casa: CATAPLANA - BIFE À CASA - ENTRECOSTO

COZINHA TRADICIONAL PORTUGUESA - **ALMOÇOS** - **JANTARES**

_____ *AR CONDICIONADO*

SANTA EULÁLIA — TELEFONE: 54852 _____ 8200 ALBUFEIRA

▶ 6 Listen to someone talking about their free time on the recording, and complete these statements by choosing the most appropriate word.

1 Gabriela likes to listen to............................... music
   a classical   **b** rock   **c** Brazilian

2 She loves going to the ....
   a theatre   **b** opera   **c** cinema

3 She goes swimming...............................
   a once a month   **b** once a week   **c** every day

4 She never...........................
   a watches TV   **b** reads   **c** does sewing

Self-evaluation

Now see if you can do the following:

a Ask someone what they like to do in their free time.
b Say what you like doing.
c Respond to someone who has asked if they can take a chair from your table.
e Say how often you watch television.
f Ask Mr and Mrs da Costa if they often listen to music.
g Say you're going to town to go shopping.

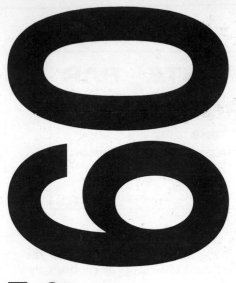

09

as férias
holidays

In this unit you will learn
- how to talk about holidays
- how to talk about where you will holiday this year / next year
- numbers 101–199
- months of the year
- how to talk about wanting to do things
- how to talk about events in the future

Leitura *Reading*

Read the following passage from a travel brochure, and then answer questions 1 to 5.

Onde é que vocês vão passar as férias este ano? Porque não passam tempo connosco na ilha do Paraíso? Temos tudo aqui para umas férias maravilhosas e relaxantes.

Podem andar nas praias douradas, nadar num mar azul-claro, ou passear no campo sossegado. Se gostam de praticar desportos, temos duas quadras de ténis, três piscinas, um campo de golfe, e desportos aquáticos. A ilha fica longe de todo o stress quotidiano, e oferece a oportunidade de se relaxar num ambiente natural e especial.

passar as férias	*to spend (the) holidays*
este ano	*this year*
connosco	*with us*
a ilha do Paraíso	*Paradise island*
tudo	*everything*
maravilhoso	*wonderful*
relaxante	*relaxing*
podem	*you (pl) can*
as praias douradas	*golden beaches*
o mar azul-claro	*clear-blue sea*
o campo sossegado	*peaceful countryside*
quadra de ténis	*tennis court*
um campo de golfe	*golf course*
desportos aquáticos	*water sports*
longe	*a long way*
quotidiano	*everyday*
oferece	*offers*
a oportunidade	*opportunity*
um ambiente natural e especial	*a natural, special atmosphere*

1 Onde pode passar umas férias maravilhosas?
2 O que pode fazer nas praias?
3 Onde pode nadar na ilha?
4 O que há para fazer se gosta de desportos?
5 O que é que a ilha oferece?

▶ Diálogo 1

Fernando is talking to a colleague about where he and his family usually spend their holidays.

Fernando Então, Júlio, vai tirar férias este ano?

Júlio Vou, sim. Vou para a Grécia. A minha mulher quer conhecer a cultura grega. E o Fernando? Onde vai?

Fernando Geralmente, viajamos pela Europa, e ficamos em vários países. Sempre gostamos de provar as comidas estrangeiras. E os seus filhos, Júlio? Vão com vocês?

Júlio Não. A minha filha nunca passa as férias connosco. Sempre vai com o namorado para a França. De vez em quando o nosso filho quer vir connosco, mas em geral prefere passar o verão na praia.

tirar férias	*to take / have a holiday*
a Grécia	*Greece*
quer	*wants*
conhecer	*to get to know*
a cultura grega	*Greek culture*
viajamos pela Europa	*we travel through Europe*
vários	*various*
(o) país	*country*
sempre	*always*
provar	*to try, taste*
comidas estrangeiras	*foreign food*
o/a namorado/a	*boy / girl friend*
a França	*France*
vir	*to come*
o verão	*summer*

Grammar

1 Two irregular verbs

A couple more irregular verbs you may want to use are **querer** (*to want*) and **vir** (*to come*). Here they are written out in the normal format:

	querer *to want*	**vir** *to come*
I	quero	venho
You (informal)	queres	vens
He/she/it/you	quer	vem
We	queremos	vimos
They/you (pl)	querem	vêm

2 Two verbs for 'to know': *saber* and *conhecer*

Both of the above verbs mean *to know*. **Saber** is used to know a fact, or how to do something. You came across an example of it in Unit 7. **Conhecer** means to know a person or place, and to get to know someone or somewhere. You would say

Sabe que horas são?	*Do you know what time it is?*
Não sei.	*I don't know.*

but

Não conheço a Áustria.	*I don't know Austria.*

Note: In the *I* (first) person, the c acquires a little tail (a cedilha) to maintain a soft-c sound.

3 Pela Europa *Through Europe*

Pela is another example of those contracted word forms you keep coming across. It comes from the preposition **por** (*through, by*) + **o, a, os, as**, the full forms being **pelo, pela, pelos, pelas**.

Pelo mar.	*Through the sea.*
Pelas ruas.	*Through the streets.*

Exercises

1 Fill in your part of the dialogue, according to the instructions. You are discussing where you and your family spend your holidays.

Teresa	Onde passa as férias em geral?
a You	*Say you often go to Italy in the spring* (**na primavera**).
Teresa	Por que gosta da Itália?
b You	*Say you like Italian culture.*
Teresa	E os filhos também vão?
c You	*Say that your son always comes with you, but that*

your daughter prefers to travel with her boyfriend.

Teresa Onde quer ir nas férias de inverno (*winter*)?

d You *Say that you usually stay at home, but that you and your family want to get to know France in the autumn (**no outono**).*

2 Choose the correct verb (**conhecer** or **saber**) to fill in the gaps in these sentences.

a Sabes que horas são? Não ___.
b A minha mãe ___ o teu irmão.
c A Paula e a Susana não ___ falar italiano.
d Vocês ___ o Brasil?
e Eu ___ nadar muito bem.
f Nós não ___ onde vamos passar as férias.

▶ Diálogo 2

Daniela and Lúcia are discussing where they would like to spend their holidays, and where they are going to spend them.

Daniela Lúcia, onde vais passar as férias este ano?

Lúcia Pois, em Março vou visitar a Inglaterra para passar tempo com a minha amiga inglesa. E tu, Daniela? Tens férias este ano?

Daniela Tenho. Vou passar quinze dias na Espanha, em Novembro. A minha mãe diz que é muito bonita no outono. O que vais fazer para o ano?

Lúcia Bom, no ano que vem gostaria de viajar pela Índia. E tu?

Daniela Também gostaria de fazer uma viagem exótica, mas não tenho muito dinheiro. Provavelmente no ano que vem vou passar as férias na terra, em Braga.

Março	*March*
quinze dias	*fifteen days (= a fortnight)*
Novembro	*November*
diz	*says*
no outono	*in the autumn*
para o ano	*next year*
no ano que vem	*next year*
gostaria de	*I would like (to)*
uma viagem exótica	*an exotic journey*
o dinheiro	*money*
provavelmente	*probably*
na terra	*in (one's) home town, region*

i The Portuguese are very attached to their home towns, especially those who come from country areas (**o campo**). Throughout history, the land (**a terra**), has played an important part in the lives of the Portuguese, as Portugal has been a predominantly agricultural country. It is not surprising, then, that the Portuguese refer to their home towns as **a terra**.

Nevertheless, they do like to travel, settling all over the world (at the last count more than 5 million Portuguese emigrants were scattered around the globe). But, despite their globetrotting, it is often to **a terra** that their feet turn when they feel **saudades** (a distinctly Portuguese feeling of the deep yearning for far-off places or people).

Grammar

▶ 1 Os meses do ano *The months of the year*

Janeiro	*January*	**Julho**	*July*
Fevereiro	*February*	**Agosto**	*August*
Março	*March*	**Setembro**	*September*
Abril	*April*	**Outubro**	*October*
Maio	*May*	**Novembro**	*November*
Junho	*June*	**Dezembro**	*December*

Note that the months in Portuguese do have capital letters, although you may find them written with small letters in Brazil.

2 Now or next year?

When you want to talk about things you do now, you use the simple parts of the verbs you have been learning – these are in the present time, i.e. what you are doing now, or what you usually do:

Sempre vou a uma aula de francês.   *I always go to a French class.*

If you want to talk about an action which is going to take place at some point in the future, be it near or far in time, you can simply use the appropriate part of the verb **ir** (*to go*), plus the action verb in exactly the same way we do in English.

Vamos visitar o Japão no ano que vem.   *We're going to visit Japan next year.*

Vou à cidade amanhã.   *I'm going to town tomorrow.*

3 Gostaria de *I would like to*

You know already how to talk about things you like, using **gostar de**. If you want to discuss something *you would like to do*, then you must use the form used by Lúcia in the dialogue: **gostaria de viajar** (*I would like to travel*). **Gostaria** is also the form for *he*, *she* and polite *you*. Add **-s** to it, and you have the form for *you* (**tu**) – **gostarias**. *We would like* is **gostaríamos**, and *they* (and *you* plural) is **gostariam**.

O que gostaria de ver?	*What would you like to see?*
Gostaríamos de comprar um carro.	*We would like to buy a car.*

Exercises

3   Make six complete sentences using the components from the columns below. There is a variety of possible answers. Take care to match the correct verb form with the correct person form. You'll find some sample answers in the **Key to the exercises** in the back of the book.

a	Eu	vamos	trabalhar	pela Escócia	amanhã
b	Tu	vão	jogar	no mar	no ano que vem
c	Você	vou	tirar	no jardim	em Julho
d	Nós	vai	visitar	golfe	na sexta-feira
e	Os senhores	vão	nadar	férias	em Abril
f	Eles	vais	viajar	o meu amigo	no sábado

4   Can you find all the months hidden in this wordsearch?

A	J	U	L	H	O	B	F	C	O
D	D	E	I	F	G	H	E	I	R
S	E	J	R	K	L	O	V	M	B
E	Z	N	B	O	H	P	E	Q	U
T	E	J	A	N	E	I	R	O	T
E	M	R	U	S	T	O	E	U	U
M	B	J	V	W	X	Y	I	Z	O
B	R	A	B	C	O	Ç	R	A	M
R	O	R	B	M	E	V	O	N	M
O	T	S	O	G	A	D	E	F	G

5   How would you say the following?

a   I would like to visit Germany.
b   Paulo would not like to work on Monday.
c   Would you (pl) like to drink with us?
d   My husband / wife would like to try Brazilian food.
e   We would like to travel through America.

Documento

For which months is this train timetable valid?

95

holidays

09

COMBOIO DE FÉRIAS

PORTO-ALGARVE-PORTO

A partir de 30 de Junho até 10 de Setembro de 200X realiza-se este serviço, com os horários e dias de circulação abaixo indicados:

20800//20801	20802//20803		ESTAÇÕES		20862//20863	20864//20865
1-2	1-2				1-2	1-2
6 30	20 45	P	Porto (Campanha)	C	0 00	8 18
6 36	20 52		Vila Nova de Gaia		23 54	8 12
6 48	21 05		Espinho		23 41	7 58
7 15	21 33		Aveiro		23 12	7 27
7 47	22 10	C	Coimbra-B	P	22 38	6 53
7 48	22 12	P	Coimbra-B	C	22 36	6 52
8 52	23 16	C	Entroncamento	P	21 29	5 41
9 04	23 30	P	Entroncamento	C	21 15	5 24
14 50	5 45	C	Tunes	P	15 10	22 47
14 54	5 53	P	Tunes	C	15 08	22 41
15 03	6 03		Albufeira		15 02	22 35
15 18	6 20		Loulé		14 45	22 18
15 32	6 35	C	Faro	P	14 29	22 01
15 47	7 05	P	Faro	C	14 10	21 29
15 57	7 14		Olhão		14 01	21 20
16 20	7 43		Tavira		13 37	20 57
10 17	8 17		V. Real de S António		13 19	20 26
16 50	8 20	C	V. R. de S. Ant.-Guad.	P	13 05	20 20

* Ligações de e para o Ramal de Lagos. Consulte os Cartazes Horários n.os 12 .

Grammar

▶ Os números 101–199 *Numbers 101–199*

If you really feel you know the numbers so far, then you'll be ready to go a bit further. You finished at 100 (**cem, cento**) last time. Here is the next group.

101	cento e um, uma	150	cento e cinquenta
102	cento e dois, duas	160	cento e sessenta
105	cento e cinco	170	cento e setenta
110	cento e dez	180	cento e oitenta
120	cento e vinte	190	cento e noventa
130	cento e trinta	199	cento e noventa e nove
140	cento e quarenta		

The pattern for the formation of these numbers is just the same as for the last group you learnt (see page 71).

cento e trinta e seis   100 + 30 + 6 = 136

Don't forget, again, wherever *one*, or *two*, appear, you must decide on the masculine or feminine form. Portuguese currency is masculine (**o euro**), so you might pay **dois euros** for a beer, but if you wanted to buy 122 beers, then you would have to ask for **cento e vinte e duas cervejas**!

▶ Let's practise some numbers and also see how many countries you can remember from earlier units. Listen to the recording and see how you get on.

Exercise

6   Say whether these sums are true (V = verdadeiro) or false (F = falso).

a   Cento e cinco + trinta e um   = cento e trinta e seis
b   Cento e noventa – vinte   = cento e quarenta
c   Setenta e dois + quinze   = cento e vinte e dois
d   Cento e sessenta – cinquenta   = cento e dez
e   Cento e oitenta e três –
        oitenta e três   = cem

Self-evaluation

See if you can now do the following:

a   ask a group of friends where they're going to spend their holidays this year.
b   say that you want to get to know Greece.
c   say that your family always spends its holidays in Portugal.
d   ask someone if they know how to swim.
e   say where you are going to spend your holiday next year.
f   ask someone if they would like to come too.
g   say the months of the year out loud.
h   pick ten numbers at random between 100 and 199, and say them out loud.

10

transportes

transport

In this unit you will learn
- how to discuss travelling and travel arrangements
- how to talk about means of transport
- the numbers from 200 upwards
- how to give some orders!
- how to say 'more than' and 'less than'

Before you begin

Before starting this unit, the last of the first part of this course, have a look back at Unit 3, Unit 7 and Unit 9 to make sure you really know the numbers up to 199.

▶ Diálogo 1

Olívia and Luísa are discussing how they travel to work. Try to follow the dialogue first by listening to your recording, and then by reading it a couple of times.

Olívia Bom dia, Luísa. Vais trabalhar hoje?
Luísa Vou, sim.
Olívia Queres uma boleia? Acho que vou passar à tua empresa.
Luísa Obrigadinha, mas não. Hoje vou primeiro ao dentista. Vou de autocarro. Depois vou a pé para o trabalho.
Olívia Muito bem. Então, até logo.

hoje	*today*
uma boleia	*a lift*
acho (que)	*I think (that)*
passar	*to pass (by)*
a empresa	*company, workplace*
obrigadinha	*thanks very much*
o dentista	*dentist*
vou de autocarro	*I'm going by bus*
vou a pé	*I'm going on foot*

▶ Diálogo 2

Now listen to Senhor Pinto answering some questions about his travel to work.

Entrevistador Senhor Pinto, como vai para o trabalho?
Sr Pinto Bem, geralmente vou de comboio. O meu trabalho fica fora da cidade, um pouco longe. Vou e volto todos os dias.
Entrevistador O senhor não tem carro?
Sr Pinto Não tenho. Queria comprar, mas não tenho dinheiro, e o comboio é rápido e barato. Viajo mais de quinhentos quilómetros por semana.
Entrevistador E vai sempre de comboio?

Sr Pinto   Às vezes vou de camioneta, e quando tenho uma reunião no Porto, vou de avião.

como vai para o trabalho?	*how do you get to work?*
vou de comboio	*I go by train*
fora da cidade	*outside the city*
longe	*far away*
vou e volto	*I go and return*
o carro	*car*
queria comprar	*I would like to buy*
rápido	*fast*
barato	*cheap*
mais de	*more than*
quinhentos quilómetros	*500 kilometres*
de camioneta	*by coach*
uma reunião	*meeting*
de avião	*by plane*

i The Portuguese have a tendency to make things appear smaller, more affectionate, or friendly. This is done by modifying the endings of words, usually adding **-inho**, or **-zinho**, among others. In the first dialogue, Luísa said **obrigadinha**, coming from the more usual **obrigada**. You will hear many people use this form of thanks. Other common words of this type you may come across include: **coitadinho(a)**, from **coitado** (*poor thing*), **um livrinho**, from **livro** (*book*), and **pãozinho** (*bread roll*), from **pão**. Conversely, some words are made larger by the addition of -**ão**; so if you want a bottle of wine (**uma garrafa de vinho**), and you asked for a **garrafão**, you'd get a five-litre flagon!

Grammar

1 De carro, a pé *By car, on foot*

Means of transport is, in the main, conveyed by **de**, plus the name of the vehicle. Thus you could travel:

▶ **de carro**	*by car*	**de barco**	*by boat*
de comboio	*by train*	**de bicicleta**	*by bike*
de autocarro	*by bus*	**de moto(cicleta)**	*by motorbike*
de camioneta	*by coach*	but **a pé**	*on foot*
de avião	*by plane, air*	**a cavalo**	*on horseback*
de metro (metropolitano)		*by underground (metro)*	

2 Quero, queria *I want, I would like*

Queria is the polite form of the verb **querer** (*to wish, want*). You learnt this verb in the last unit. **Queria** is what you would use to ask for anything in a shop, ticket office, café, and so on. However, you also hear many Portuguese people using the present form of the verb, especially on offering food or drinks, where in English you would probably use the polite form.

> Quer comer alguma coisa?   *Do you want to eat anything?*
> (i.e. *would you like to?*)

3 Mais de, menos de *More than, less than*

In Unit 4, you used **mais** (*more*) and **menos** (*less*) when talking about people being taller, shorter, older than each other. When discussing numbers – be it prices, distances, time – *more*, or *less than*, is expressed by **mais de** and **menos de**.

> Mais de cinquenta libras.   *More than £50.00*
> Menos de dez minutos.   *Less than ten minutes.*

▶ 4 Os números 200 + *Numbers 200+*

If you are going to discuss distances you will need to be confident with numbers into the thousands. Who knows, if you played the **totoloto**, you could end up winning thousands of euros – and who's going to count it if you can't? So, to help you on your way, here is the final group of numbers, from 200.

200	duzentos	**1,000**	mil
300	trezentos	**2,000**	dois mil
400	quatrocentos	**10,000**	dez mil
500	quinhentos	**100,000**	cem mil
600	seiscentos	**1,000,000**	um milhão
700	setecentos		
800	oitocentos		
900	novecentos		

You can help yourself to learn numbers by looking for pattern-groups.

5 cinco	15 quinze	50 cinquenta	500 quinhentos
8 oito	18 dezoito	80 oitenta	800 oitocentos.

The numbers in the 100s (200, 300, 400, and so on) also have a feminine form, to be used when talking about large numbers of feminine items. If you wanted to say 400 miles, you'd have to use **quatrocent*as*** with **milh*as***.

The digits which make up the hundreds, tens, and units, are, in the main, divided in the same way as the last group you learnt – with the word **e** between each one. Hence, 953 would be: **novecentos e cinquenta e três**.

After thousands, there is usually no **e**. It only appears if the thousand is followed either by a numeral from 1 to 100, or by a numeral from 200 to 900 if the last two numbers are zeros.

1996 = **mil novecentos e noventa e seis**
2003 = **dois mil e três**

Don't be daunted by numbers. Take every opportunity to practise them, and listen carefully when people tell you prices. When in doubt, you can always ask them to write things down.

Podia escrevê-lo?   *Could you write it?*

Exercises

1   Fill in the gaps in this monologue, choosing from the words listed.

Em ___ vou para o trabalho ___ autocarro. Vou e ___ todos os ___ . O autocarro é ___ e bastante (*quite*) ___ . Nos ___ de semana viajo ___ da cidade. ___ de comboio. Aos domingos ___ de passear de ___ . Quando vou de ___ , viajo de ___ ou de ___ .

volto	rápido	vou	férias
geral	dias	fins	gosto
avião	de	barato	fora
bicicleta	barco		

▶ **Actividade dois: 2** Listen to the list of numbers on your recording, and see if you can repeat each one, and then write down what you think each number is.

AUTOCARROS. Rua da República, 135. Tel. 23747/ 29624.

COMBOIOS. Tel. 22125.

TÁXI-AÉREO. Aeródromo de Évora. Tel. 28335.

Documento

Which of the telephone numbers would you ring for information about buses?

Leitura *Reading*

Read this advertisement from a sales section of a newspaper, and try answering the questions following it.

Vende-se bicicleta

Quer melhorar a sua vida? Está farto de viajar no carro dos seus amigos, ou de pedir boleia aos seus pais? Tenho uma bicicleta bonita que você vai querer comprar. Com uma bicicleta, pode-se passear no campo, chegar mais rápido ao trabalho, e melhorar a saúde. Só custa vinte euros. É barata! É bonita! É sua! Compre já!

1 O que é que a pessoa quer vender?

2 Como é?

3 O que se pode fazer com ela?

4 Quanto custa?

5 É barata, ou cara?

vende-se bicicleta	*bicycle for sale*
melhorar	*to improve*
a vida	*life*
estar farto de	*to be sick of*
pedir boleia	*to hitch a lift*
os pais	*parents*
comprar	*to buy*
pode-se	*one can, you can*
a saúde	*health*
só custa	*it only costs*
compre já!	*buy now!*

Grammar

1 More uses for reflexive verbs

Back in Unit 7 you learnt some verbs, known as reflexives, where the word 'self' was included with the verb (I *wash myself*, and so on). You will also find this kind of verb used in two more different situations: firstly, when something is for sale, rent, on offer, and so on. Often the signs you see will say **vende-se** (*for sale*), **aluga-se** (*for rent*) or **oferece-se** (*on offer*). In the bike advertisement (in the **Reading** passage) what is actually being stated is that the bike 'sells itself', i.e. the actual vendor is not mentioned. You will also come across signs in shops or hotels which state **aqui fala-se inglês e francês** (*English and French are spoken here*).

Secondly, **pode-se** means *one can* (i.e. you can – it is possible), again an unspecific, non-personalized form of the verb. Pode-se fumar? **Can one smoke?**

2 De carro, no carro de X *By car, in X's car*

Remember that transport is expressed by the word **de**. However, if you want to specify either someone's vehicle, or a timetabled train, bus, plane and so on, you will use **em** (**no, na**).

no carro dos seus amigos	*in your friends' car*
no comboio das dez e meia	*on the 10.30 train*
no avião de TAP	*on the TAP plane*

3 Compre! *Buy!*

Ordering people to do things (however politely) can be rather confusing in Portuguese, so for the moment just have a brief look at the polite (you) form. With regular verbs look at what happens. Here are three examples:

Infinitive		Present tense		Polite command	
comprar	*to buy*	compra	*he, she, you buy(s)*	compre!	*buy!*
comer	*to eat*	come	*he, she, you eat(s)*	coma!	*eat!*
partir	*to leave*	parte	*he, she, you leave(s)*	parta!	*leave!*

Have you noticed the pattern? The **-ar** verbs change to an **-e** ending, and the **-er** and **-ir** verbs change the other way, to an **-a**. To order more than one person, simply add an **-m** to the above forms (**comprem, comam, partam**).

Irregular verbs are awkward. Here are a few examples:

Infinitive		Singular	Plural	
fazer	*to make / do*	faça!	façam!	*make! / do!*
ser	*to be*	seja!	sejam!	*be!*
estar	*to be*	esteja!	estejam!	*be!*
ter	*to have*	tenha!	tenham!	*have!*
ir	*to go*	vá!	vão!	*go!*
vir	*to come*	venha!	venham!	*come!*

You will pick up on other examples as you go along. In English these commands are usually followed by an extra word – more to give weight and rhythm to the command than for meaning. For example: *Have it! Go on / away! Come here!* Portuguese does the same: **Tome lá! Vá embora! Venha cá!**

Exercises

3 How would you say the following?

a I go to work in my friend's car.
b Paulo goes to the hospital by bus.
c Ana is travelling on the 2.30 p.m. train.
d Mr and Mrs da Costa are going on holiday by boat.
e We are going to the cinema on the 7.15 p.m. bus.
f Are you (**tu**) travelling by plane?

4 Supply the correct command forms to complete these sentences.

a (comprar – singular) ___ o carro!
b (comer – plural) ___ as sardinhas!
c (partir – plural) ___ hoje!
d (viajar – singular) ___ de comboio!
e (falar – plural) ___ menos rápido!
f (beber – singular) ___ o café!

▶ 5 Listen to six people describing how they tend to travel, and put the list of transports in order, according to who said them.

[ ] bicycle [ ] car [ ] on foot [ ] horse [ ] coach [ ] bus

Self-evaluation

You have now completed the first ten units of the course, which have given you the basics of the Portuguese language. You have covered a lot of material, and before you go on to use your knowledge in the practical situations in the second part of the book, try this revision exercise to make sure you have all the information you need firmly established.

Can you:

a   ask someone their name?
b   say pleased to meet you?
c   tell someone your nationality, and say where you are from?
d   say that your husband / wife speaks Portuguese?
e   ask a couple where they live?
f   tell your friends where you work, and what your occupation is?
g   say how old you are?
h   describe someone in your family?
i   ask someone if they like coffee?
j   say that you prefer France?
k   describe your house?
l   say where your sofa / table / wardrobe is?
m   ask what the time is?
n   describe your daily routine?
o   ask a couple if they like to travel?
p   say what you like doing in your free time?
q   ask someone where they spend their holidays?
r   say that you and your family would like to visit Spain?
s   ask someone how they get to work?
t   count to a million!?

So, how did you get on? If you managed to answer 15 or more confidently, then **Parabéns!** and on you go to Unit 11. If you were unsure of any of these questions revise the units which contain the points you may have got stuck on. Work through the exercises again, and use your recording, until you are happy to move on.

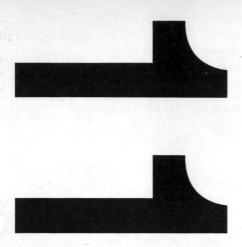

11

viajar
travelling

In this unit you will learn
- how to talk about using public transport
- how to buy tickets
- how to get information at the tourist office
- how to ask for and understand directions

Before you begin

Travelling on public transport in Portugal is an interesting option, and it is generally cheap and efficient as well as a way of seeing more of the country and its people. Once you have learnt a few basic phrases for travelling, you will have a lot more confidence to get about.

▶ Diálogos

Listen, then read out loud the following short exchanges taking place at various departure points for different means of transport.

No aeroporto *At the airport*

Senhor	Faz favor, há autocarros para o centro da cidade?
Informações	Sim, há. O senhor sai do aeroporto e a paragem é ali em frente. Também pode tomar um táxi. A praça de táxis é lá fora.

No porto *At the port*

Senhora	Desculpe, a que horas parte o barco para Madeira?
Senhor	Às dez e quinze.
Senhora	E a que horas chega?
Senhor	Às quatro menos vinte da manhã.

Na rua (1) *In the street*

Senhora	Faz favor, há uma estação de comboios aqui?
Senhor	Sim, a estação de caminho de ferro é ali, à esquerda.

Na rua (2)

Senhor	Onde é a paragem de autocarros para Lagos?
Senhora	É ali, à direita. Também pode apanhar um autocarro do terminal, que é ali atrás da praça.

Num táxi *In a taxi*

Turista	Para o hotel Vistamar, se faz favor.
Taxista	Muito bem.
Turista	Quanto é?
Taxista	São sete euros.

a cidade	town / city
o centro	centre
o senhor sai	you leave / go out
a paragem	(bus) stop
ali / lá	there
tomar	to take
a praça de táxis	taxi rank
lá fora	out there
o porto	port
parte	departs
chega	arrives
a estação de comboios	train station
a estação de caminho de ferro (C.F.)	railway station
à esquerda	on / to the left
à direita	on / to the right
apanhar	to catch (bus)
o terminal	bus terminus
para	to / for
o hotel	hotel
quanto é?	how much is it?
são . . . euros	it's . . . euros

Exercise

1 How would you say the following?

a Are there buses to Lisbon (Lisboa)?
b The bus stop is over there on the left.
c The taxi rank is there on the right.
d What time does the train for Faro leave?
e At 6.15 in the evening.
f What time does the boat arrive?
g Is there an airport here?
h The bus terminus is over there, in front.
i To the port please.

▶ Diálogo 6

Ana quer viajar de comboio. *Ana wants to travel by train.*

Ana Bom dia. Queria um bilhete para o Porto, se faz favor.
Senhor Quer de ida ou de ida e volta?
Ana Ida e volta.
Senhor Primeira ou segunda classe?
Ana Segunda faz favor. É um rápido?
Senhor Há um rápido-directo às duas horas.
Ana Qual é a linha?
Senhor É a linha número quatro.
Ana Obrigada.
Senhor De nada, bom dia.

um bilhete	*ticket*
de ida / ida e volta	*single / return*
um rápido (-directo)	*express (direct)*
muito bem	*very well*
qual?	*which?*
a linha	*platform*
de nada	*don't mention it*

i Travelling by train in Portugal is extremely cheap and trains usually run on time. There is a variety of tariffs depending on when you travel: most stations have information leaflets (**folhetos de informação**) with timetables (**horários**) and prices (**preços**).

You can also travel by coach (**camioneta**). The long-distance coaches are very luxurious. You can usually only buy a single ticket, (**simples**) and you have to buy another single at the coach station (**central rodoviária/central de camionagem**) on your return.

Exercise

▶ 2 **Actividade dois:** Fill in your part of this dialogue, according to the instructions in italics.

Na estação de caminho de ferro. *At the railway station.*

a **You** *Say good afternoon, I'd like two tickets to Loulé, please.*

	Senhor	Quer de ida ou de ida e volta?
b	You	*Return, please.*
	Senhor	Primeira ou segunda classe?
c	You	*First. Which platform is it to Loulé?*
	Senhor	É a linha número um.
d	You	*What time does the train leave?*
	Senhor	Às oito menos dez.
e	You	*And what time does it arrive?*
	Senhor	Às nove e vinte e cinco.
f	You	*Thank you.*
	Senhor	De nada. Boa tarde.

Documento

a Is the ticket on the right a single or return?

b Is the ticket below 1st or 2nd class?

Caminhos de Ferro Portugueses

TUNES
ALCANTARILHA

Preço	2a classe	Inteiro
€ 5,85		Adulto

EVA Turismo

BILHETE SIMPLES
No: 18005 J

Tarifa: Euros – 7,50

De: Braga
Para: Coimbra

Conserve este bilhete

IVA INCLUÍDO

▶ Diálogo

No turismo *At the tourist office*

Turista Tem uma lista de hotéis da cidade?

Senhora Aqui tem uma lista de hotéis, pensões e albergues. Também há um parque de campismo nos arredores da cidade.

Turista E tem uma planta da cidade?

Senhora Temos esta, e um mapa da região.

Turista E tem informações sobre a cidade, as lojas, as atracções…?

Senhora Aqui tem.

tem . . . ?	*do you have?*
uma lista	*a list*
hotéis (um hotel)	*hotels (hotel)*
pensões (uma pensão)	*guest houses (guest house)*
albergues	*hostels*
um parque de campismo	*campsite*
nos arredores	*on the outskirts*
uma planta	*town plan*
um mapa	*map*
a região	*region*
informações	*information*
as lojas	*shops*
as atracções	*attractions*

Leitura *Reading*

Read the following extract from a tourist information leaflet, and see how much you can understand. Use the vocabulary box that follows it to help you get the gist.

Albufeira
Típica cidade de pescadores. Ambiente jovem. Praias entre rochedos e falésias de cor vermelha.

Armação de Pêra
Areal extenso. Próximo pequenas praias tranquilas. Centro turístico.

Gastronomia
Deliciosos pratos de peixe e mariscos. Destaque especial para as suculentas cataplanas e as sardinhas assadas. Doces de amêndoa e figo. A cozinha internacional de qualidade.

Quinta do Lago
Complexo turístico. Lago artificial. Extenso areal. Campo de golfe.

Silves
Capital do Algarve durante a ocupação árabe e até ao século XVI. Interessante castelo e catedral gótica.

Vinho
O solo algarvio, aquecido pelo sol, produz vinhos brancos e tintos aveludados. O vinho de Lagoa ja ganhou renome mundial.

típico(a)	*typical*
pescadores	*fishermen*
ambiente	*atmosphere*
jovem	*young*
rochedos e falésias de cor vermelha	*red cliffs and crags*
areal extenso	*long stretch of sandy beach*
próximo	*nearby*
tranquilas	*calm*
deliciosos pratos	*delicious dishes*
destaque especial para	*special emphasis on*
suculentas	*tasty*
cataplanas	*cataplana-cooked dishes*
sardinhas assadas	*grilled sardines*
doces de amêndoa e figo	*almond and fig sweets*
a cozinha	*cuisine*
lago artificial	*artificial lake*
campo de golfe	*golf course*
durante	*during*
a ocupação árabe	*the Arab occupation*
o século	*century*
catedral gótica	*gothic cathedral*
o solo algarvio	*the Algarve ground / soil*
aquecido pelo sol	*warmed by the sun*
produz	*produces*
aveludados	*velvet-like*
já ganhou renome mundial	*has already won world acclaim*

Exercise

3 Can you answer these questions on the information contained in the **folheto**?

a Armação de Pêra é bom para os turistas?
b O que há em Silves?
c Qual é a comida típica do Algarve?
d Onde se pode jogar golfe?
e O Algarve produz vinho verde?
f Que tipo de cidade é Albufeira?

▶ Diálogos

Read and listen to the following dialogues and at the same time look at the town centre map. There is a vocabulary box after the dialogues.

À porta do turismo *Outside the tourist office*

Senhor   Faz favor, onde fica a estação de caminho de ferro?
Transeunte O senhor vira aqui à esquerda, toma a segunda rua à direita, segue sempre em frente, e a estação fica à esquerda.

Na praça *In the town square*

Senhora Desculpe, sabe onde fica o banco?
Senhor   Sim. O banco é muito perto daqui. Siga sempre em frente até ao correio, depois vire à esquerda, e o banco é ali à esquina.

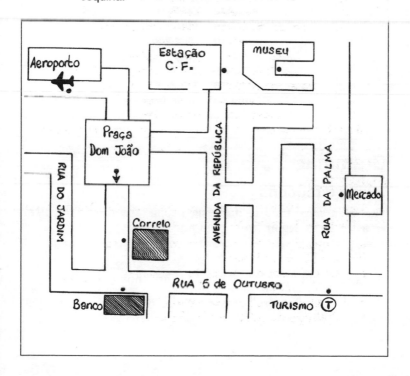

▶ No mercado *At the market*

Isabel   Nuno, tu sabes onde fica o museu?
Nuno   Sim. É muito fácil. Vai lá fora, vira à direita, e segue sempre em frente. Toma a terceira à esquerda e o museu fica mesmo ali em frente.

(onde) fica	*(where) is situated*
transeunte	*passer-by*
lá fora	*(there) outside*
vira, vire	*turn*
toma	*take*
a rua	*road*
segue, siga em frente	*carry straight on*
o banco	*bank*
perto (daqui)	*near (here)*
até (a)	*until / up to*
o correio	*post office*
à esquina	*on the corner*
sabe, sabes	*you know*
o museu	*museum*
fácil	*easy*
vai	*go*
terceira	*third*
mesmo ali	*right there*

Grammar

Giving directions

The main verbs used in directing people are: **tomar** (*to take*), **virar** (*to turn*), **seguir** (*to follow*) and **ir** (*to go*).

Toma a segunda rua.   *You take the second road.*

Vire aqui à esquerda.   *Turn* (polite) *left there.*

Depending on how well you know the person the verb-endings may well differ.

	Very polite	Polite (Você)	Familiar (Tu)
o senhor a senhora }	toma vira segue vai	tome vire siga vá	toma vira segue vai

The last two columns are known as commands. As you will mainly be listening to directions, the main thing to focus on is understanding the direction, and not worry too much about the verb ending at this stage.

Exercises

4 Look at the map again on page 113 and see if you could give directions (in the polite form) to the following places (in each case imagine you are standing outside the starting point with your back to it).

a from the **turismo** to the **banco**
b from the **correio** to the **mercado**
c from the **museu** to the **estação**
d from the **aeroporto** to the **Turismo**

5 Now follow these directions and see if you can discover where you have been sent.

a Start at the **museu**: Siga em frente e vire à direita. Depois vá em frente e o _____ fica à esquerda.
b Start at the **banco**: Vá lá fora e vire à direita. Tome a primeira à esquerda e siga sempre em frente, até à _____ que fica à esquerda.
c Start at the **estação**: Vire à direita e vá sempre em frente. Tome a segunda à esquerda. Depois siga sempre em frente e o _____ fica à direita.

▶ 6 Listen to the instructions given in the dialogue on the recording, and fill in the correct directions below.

Faz favor, onde fica ....?

Bem, a senhora .... aqui ...., e .... a .... rua .... até ...., e .... fica ....

Obrigada.

12

na cidade
in town

In this unit you will learn
- how to exchange money
- how to buy stamps and make phone calls
- how to recognize a few public signs
- how to find a toilet in Portugal!

Before you begin

You are going to come across a lot of numbers in this unit. This will be excellent practice. However, you might want to revise the numbers in Units 3, 7, 9 and 10.

▶ Diálogo

No banco *In the bank*

Senhora	Posso levantar dinheiro com o meu cartão aqui? A máquina está avariada.
Clerk	Com certeza. Quanto queria?
Senhora	100 (cem) euros, se faz favor.
Clerk	Um momento, sim? Tem passaporte?
Senhora	Aqui está.
Clerk	Faça favor de preencher este formulário: nome, morada aqui em Portugal, número do cartão.
Senhora	Já está.
Clerk	Ora bem. [counting the money] 20 (vinte), 40 (quarenta), 60 (sessenta), 80 (oitenta), 100 (cem) euros.
Senhora	Obrigada.
Clerk	De nada. Bom dia.

levantar	*to take out, withdraw money*
o dinheiro	*money*
o cartão	*card*
a máquina	*machine*
avariada	*broken down*
com certeza	*of course, certainly*
quanto . . . ?	*How much . . . ?*
um momento	*one moment*
o passaporte	*passport*
faça favor de . . .	*please . . .*
preencher	*fill in, complete*
este formulário	*this form*
a morada	*address*
já está	*there we are, there it is* (lit. *already it is*)
ora bem	*right then*

i You won't have any problems finding a bank in Portugal. Many of the larger towns and tourist areas have modern banks, with services such as the **multibanco** (ATM) machines. Inside the bank look for the exchange sign (**câmbio**) on the counter. Sometimes you are handed a small disc with a number on it, known as **uma chapa**. You need to take this to the **caixa** and wait for your number to be called; they will then deal with your cash. Portugal uses the euro: it is masculine word (**o euro**), and is divided into 100 **cêntimos**.

▶ Diálogo

No correio *At the post office*

Sandra	Olá, queria oito selos para Inglaterra, e dois para Alemanha, se faz favor.
Senhora	São para cartas, ou postais?
Sandra	Três cartas e sete postais.
Senhora	Bom, são seis euros ao todo.
Sandra	Queria fazer uma chamada também.
Senhora	Quer passar para a cabine um.
Sandra	Obrigada.

um selo	*stamp*
para cartas / postais	*for letters / postcards*
ao todo	*in total, all*
fazer uma chamada	*to make a phonecall*
passar	*to pass*
a cabine	*booth*

Exercise

1 Match up the questions with the replies underneath.

   i   Qual é a sua morada aqui em Portugal?
   ii   Para cartas, ou postais?
   iii Queria fazer uma chamada.
   iv Posso levantar dinheiro?
   v   Tem passaporte?

   a   Quer passar para a cabine três.
   b   É o apartamento Sol, Praça São João, Loulé.
   c   Claro. Quanto queria?
   d   Para cinco cartas.
   e   Aqui está.

i Making phone calls from Portugal can be very expensive. Calls from your hotel, or from the post office, are always at an inflated rate. If you have to call home, find a telephone box (**uma cabine telefónica**) – many are now operated by telephone cards (**um cartão telefónico**) available at post offices, newsagents and stree kiosks. They are sold in multiples of euros (5, 10, 20).

i Public signs and notices

Can you guess what any of the following signs mean in English? (Answers in the **Key to the exercises** at the back of the book.)

a PARA CRIANÇAS	e PERIGO
b NÃO FUMAR	f SAÍDA DE EMERGÊNCIA
c PROIBIDO ESTACIONAR	g ENTRADA PROIBIDA
d ABERTO DAS 10.00 ÀS 12.00	h FECHADO

Documento

Look at the following sign and answer the questions on it.

Proibido Estacionar
entre as 13:00 e as
15:00 horas.

Saída de Emergência
Lojas Primavera.

a What can you not do here?
b Why?

ℹ️ Toilets!

Public conveniences are difficult to find in Portugal. It is common practice to use the toilet in a bar, café (where you may need to get the key first) or even hotel. There are various names for toilets:

a casa de banho	*bathroom*	**sanita**	*toilet bowl*
os sanitários	*public loos*	**os lavabos**	*washroom and toilet*
a retrete	*separate toilet*		

Exercise

2 Find the missing words from each phrase below, and fit them onto the crossword grid.

1 Duzentas libras ___ .
2 Tem ___ ?
3 Qual é a sua ___ em Portugal?
4 Sete ___ para Espanha, por favor.
5 10 ___ ao todo.
6 Posso ___ dinheiro?
7 Para ___ ou postais?
8 ___ número dois.

► Now take part in a dialogue at a Post Office. Listen to the prompts on the recording and speak in the pauses. You will hear the correct version afer each pause.

13

ir às compras

going shopping

In this unit you will learn
- how to buy produce at a market
- how to deal with shops
- how to get by in shopping centres

Before you begin

Shopping in Portugal can be a great learning experience, and lots of fun, especially if you look for fresh produce at the market (**o mercado**), or if you try haggling for a bargain (**uma pechincha**) at the weekly or monthly market (**a feira**). Larger cities now have supermarket chains (**os supermercados**), as well as shopping centres (**os centros comerciais**), hypermarkets (**hipermercados**), and all towns have at least a few **minimercados**. However, to practise the language, you need to venture into the smaller shops (**as lojas**), where you will have direct contact with the Portuguese people. So, **vamos às compras!**

▶ Diálogo

No mercado *At the market*

Listen to the dialogue and then read it in the book.

Senhora Silva Bom dia, minha senhora. Tem laranjas hoje?
Vendedora Tenho, sim. Quantas quer?
Senhora Silva Dê-me dois quilos se faz favor. E há cenouras?
Vendedora Há, sim.
Senhora Silva Bom, pois, eu quero meio quilo.
Vendedora Que mais?
Senhora Silva Também queria umas pêras. Estão boas hoje?
Vendedora Estão boas, mas um pouco maduras.
Senhora Silva Ah, maduras não quero. Está bem, então é tudo.

laranjas	*oranges*	**meio quilo**	*½ kilo*
hoje	*today*	**que mais?**	*what else?*
quantas?	*how many?*	**pêras**	*pears*
dê-me	*give me*	**maduras**	*ripe*
quilos	*kilos*	**é tudo**	*that's all*
cenouras	*carrots*		

Vocabulary

If you are buying produce at the market, you may need some of the following vocabulary.

Legumes	vegetables	Frutas	fruit
(as) cenouras	carrots	(as) laranjas	oranges
(as) batatas	potatoes	(as) pêras	pears
(o) repolho	cabbage	(os) morangos	strawberries
(a) couve-flor	cauliflower	(as) bananas	bananas
(o) alho-porro	leek	(o) limão	lemon
(o) pimentão	green pepper	(o) melão	melon
(os) tomates	tomatoes	(a) melancia	watermelon
(as) cebolas	onions	(o) ananás	pineapple
(os) cogumelos	mushrooms	(as) ameixas	plums
(a) alface	lettuce	(as) maçãs	apples
Peixe	fish	**Carne**	meat
(o) atum	tuna	(a) carne de porco	pork
(a) sardinha	sardine	(a) carne de vaca	beef
(o) carapau	mackerel	(o) peru	turkey
(o) bacalhau	salted cod	(o) frango	chicken
(o) peixe-espada	scabbard	(a) carne de vitela	veal
(o) espadarte	swordfish	(o) cabrito	kid
(a) pescada	hake	(o) javali	wild-boar
(o) linguado	sole	(o) leitão	suckling pig
(os) mariscos	seafood	(o) fígado	liver
(as) lulas	squid	(as) tripas	tripe

When buying meat, you might need some names of different cuts:

(a) costeleta	chop
(o) escalope	scallop (thick sliced)
(o) entrecosto	entrecôte
(a) fatia	slice (thin)
um quarto	a joint
uma asa	a wing
uma coxa	chicken drumstick / thigh

And don't forget your weights (in metric of course!)

▶ um quilo de	a kilo of	250 gramas de	250 g of
meio quilo de	half a kilo of	100 gramas de	100 g of

Wordsearch

Can you find the names of ten items of fresh produce on this grid?

M	E	L	A	N	C	I	A	A	B
C	U	A	P	A	R	A	C	D	E
F	G	E	I	H	I	J	K	S	L
M	R	N	M	M	P	Q	A	R	J
A	S	R	E	P	O	L	H	O	A
N	T	U	N	V	U	W	X	Y	V
A	Z	A	T	L	B	C	D	E	A
N	F	G	A	J	N	A	R	A	L
A	H	I	O	J	K	L	M	N	I
B	E	S	P	A	D	A	R	T	E

▶ Diálogo

Na mercearia *In the grocer's shop*

Freguesa	Boa tarde, senhor Maurício, como está?
Senhor Maurício	Bem, obrigado. E a senhora?
Freguesa	Estou bem. Olhe, preciso de comprar algumas coisas.
Senhor Maurício	Então, diga lá.
Freguesa	Quero meia dúzia de ovos, um litro de leite magro, um pacote de manteiga e uma garrafa de azeite.
Senhor Maurício	O azeite só temos desta qualidade; o mais barato acabou-se ontem.
Freguesa	Não faz mal. Levo este. Tem flambre?
Senhor Maurício	Temos este, que é muito bom, e também temos este presunto aqui.
Freguesa	Pode cortar-me cinco fatias deste presunto aqui? E quanto é aquele queijo lá ao fundo?
Senhor Maurício	Aquele queijo da Serra custa sete euros e cinquenta o quilo.
Freguesa	Ah, então, dê-me trezentos gramas por favor.
Senhor Maurício	Mais alguma coisa?
Freguesa	É só. Obrigada. Quanto é?
Senhor Maurício	Ora bem, são cinco euros e cinquenta ao todo.

freguesa	*customer*
olhe	*look*
preciso de	*I need to*
comprar	*to buy*
algumas coisas	*some things*
diga lá	*tell (me) then*
mela dúzia	*half a dozen*
ovos	*eggs*
um litro	*litre*
leite (magro)	*(skimmed) milk*
um pacote	*packet*
manteiga	*butter*
uma garrafa	*bottle*
azeite	*olive oil*
qualidade	*quality*
o mais barato	*the cheaper (one)*
acabou-se	*ran out (finished)*
ontem	*yesterday*
não faz mal	*don't worry*
fiambre	*boiled ham*
presunto	*smoked ham*
queijo (da Serra)	*(Serra) cheese*
ao fundo	*at the back*
custa	*costs*
mais alguma coisa?	*anything else?*

Vocabulary

Here are some more everyday items you may need at the grocer's:

(o) pão (de forma)	*bread (sliced)*
(a) geléia	*jam*
(as) bolachas	*biscuits*
(as) ervilhas	*peas*
(os) fósforos	*matches*
(a) pasta de dentes	*toothpaste*
(o) mel	*honey*
(a) água	*water*
(o) bolo	*cake*
(a) sopa	*soup*
(o) sabão	*soap*
(o) papel higiénico	*toilet paper*

You will also need the following vocabulary:

uma caixa (de)	a box (of)	**um frasco**	a jar
uma garrafa	bottle	**um garrafão**	demi-john
uma lata	tin, can	**uma barra**	bar
um pacote	packet	**um tubo**	tube
um rolo	roll	**um pote**	pot, jar

Exercise

1   Alice has got her shopping list in a muddle, so her items and quantities are jumbled. Can you match the items correctly?

um quilo de	*presunto*
3 costeletas de	*água*
6 fatias de	*cenouras*
um pacote de	*bolachas*
2 latas de	*pasta de dentes*
uma garrafa de	*porco*
um tubo de	*sopa*
uma dúzia de	*ovos*

Documento

Mandy wanted to buy some tuna. Did she get any? Check her till receipt to see if she bought some.

```
   SUPERMERCADO SILVA
LARGO DE SANTA MARIA, 26
7645 VILA NOVA MILFONTES
   CONT. N.801661528

  C   1     SCONTR    367
                      EUROS
AGUA CRUZE 17%         0,37
ATUM CALVO 17%         0,55
       2      X 0,40
IOG. PEDAC. 17%        0,80
PLANTA 250 17%         1,67
**TOTAL**             3,39
NUMERARIO             5,00
TROCO                1,61

CAIXA 3    UNID      5
       O B R I G A D O

   07—08—2008  17:05
```

▶ Leitura *Reading*

Listen to this passage all about buying clothes and then read it carefully in the book. Use the word box at the end only if you really get stuck.

Em Portugal há vários lugares onde se pode comprar roupa; da feira ao centro comercial e às casas de modas. As roupas e os sapatos portugueses são muito elegantes. Na Casa de Modas Silvana há roupas para homens (calças, camisas, gravatas, jaquetas) e para mulheres (vestidos, blusas, saias, conjuntos), como também os bonitos sapatos, sandálias e botas que estão na moda. Há roupas em vários estilos, cores e tamanhos. A senhora Ferreira quer comprar uma blusa. Ela procura um padrão de que gosta e pergunta se pode experimentar. Quando sai da cabine de provas pergunta se há a mesma blusa num tamanho maior, e em verde. Ela não gosta muito da azul. Há muitas cores – vermelho, amarelo, rosa, branco, preto e laranja, além de azul-claro e verde-escuro. A senhora Ferreira escolhe uma blusa em preto, depois experimenta um par de sapatos de salto alto, de cabedal. Ela calça o número 39, e os sapatos servem-lhe perfeitamente.

vários lugares	*various places*
da . . . ao	*. . . from the . . . to the . . .*
a casa de modas	*fashion house*
os sapatos	*shoes*
elegantes	*elegant*
roupas para . . .	*clothes for*
homens / mulheres	*men / women*
calças	*trousers*
camisas	*shirts*
gravatas	*ties*
jaquetas	*jackets*
vestidos	*dresses*
blusas	*blouses*
saias	*skirts*
conjuntos	*suits*
como também	*as well as*
sandálias	*sandals*
botas	*boots*
na moda	*in fashion*
estilos, padrão	*styles, style*

cores	*colours*
tamanhos	*sizes*
para si	*for herself*
procura	*she is looking for*
experimentar	*to try on*
sai	*she leaves*
a cabine de provas	*changing room*
pergunta	*she asks*
a mesma blusa	*the same blouse*
maior	*bigger*
em verde	*in green*
azul	*blue*
vermelho	*red*
amarelo	*yellow*
rosa	*pink*
branco	*white*
preto	*black*
laranja	*orange*
além de	*as well as*
azul-claro	*light blue*
verde-escuro	*dark green*
escolhe	*she chooses*
experimenta	*she tries (on)*
um par	*a pair*
de salto alto	*high heeled*
de cabedal	*in leather*
calça	*she takes (shoes)*
o número 39	*size 39*
servem-lhe perfeitamente	*fit her perfectly*

Exercises

2 Can you answer these questions based on the **Reading** passage?

a Onde se podem comprar roupas em Portugal?
b Os sapatos portugueses são elegantes?
c Há roupas para crianças na Casa Silvana?
d O que quer comprar a senhora Ferreira?
e De que cor é a blusa que ela experimenta?
f Ela escolhe que cor?
g Que tipo de sapatos experimenta?
h Ela gosta ou não?

▶ 3   **Actividade três:** Fill in your part of this dialogue in a grocer's shop.

Senhor Renato	Bom dia!
a You	*Say hello. I would like a litre of water and a loaf of sliced bread.*
Senhor Renato	Só temos este pão.
b You	*That's all right. I'll take one. Do you have smoked ham?*
Senhor Renato	Sim, temos este, que é bom.
c You	*Well, can you cut me six slices, please?*
Senhor Renato	Que mais?
d You	*I also want a tin of peas and a bar of soap.*
Senhor Renato	Mais?
e You	*That's all, thanks. How much is it?*

▶ 4   Listen to various people on the recording doing their shopping. Complete the grid below with the item they purchase, the quantity, and how much it costs. You will hear the answers on the recording.

Person	Name of item	Quantity	Price
1			
2			
3			
4			
5			

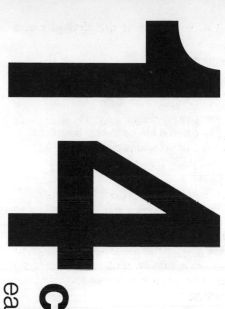

14

comer fora

eating out

In this unit you will learn
- how to order food in a café or restaurant
- something about typical Portuguese food and drink
- how to interpret menus

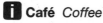 Diálogo

Na pastelaria *At the cake shop*

Paulo e os amigos entram na pastelaria Suíça.
Paulo and his friends go into the Suiça cake shop.

Empregado   Boa tarde, que desejam?
Paulo   Pois, para mim, um galão e um pastel de bacalhau.
Nuno   Eu queria uma bica e uma sandes de queijo.
Empregado   E para a menina?
Maria   Tem pastéis de nata?
Empregado   Temos, sim.
Maria   Então dê-me dois, se faz favor.
Empregado   E para beber?
Maria   Um sumo de laranja.
Empregado   Mais alguma coisa?
Paulo   Pode ser também um quarto de água mineral.
Empregado   Com ou sem gás?
Paulo   Sem, e fresca. Obrigado.
Empregado   Muito bem.

a pastelaria	*café / cake shop*
um galão	*milky coffee*
um pastel de bacalhau	*cod / potato fish cake*
uma bica	*small black coffee*
uma sandes	*sandwich*
pastéis de nata	*custard cakes*
um sumo de laranja	*fresh orange juice*
mais alguma coisa?	*anything else?*
um quarto	*¹/₄ litre bottle*
com	*with*
sem	*without*
fresca	*cooled*

ℹ Café *Coffee*

In Portugal there are many types of coffee – from small and black, to large and milky, with dozens in between! To ensure you get the better quality coffee, and not the re-cycled beans, ask for **café 'de máquina'**. Here are some of the most popular coffee drinks.

uma bica / um café	*small black espresso*
uma italiana	*espresso but only half-full (very strong)*

um garoto	*small white coffee*
um pingado / um pingo	*small with one drop of milk*
um café com leite /	*white, normal size*
uma meia de leite	
um galão	*milky coffee (served in a glass)*

Exercise

1 The waiter has brought a tray of snacks and drinks to the table but has forgotten who ordered what. Can you help him to sort it out?

What did each person ask for?

a Paulo wants a black coffee, ham sandwich and custard cake.

b Nuno wants a milky coffee, cheese sandwich, cod cake and custard cake.

c Ana wants a black coffee, ham sandwich and two cod cakes.

d Maria wants a small slightly milky coffee, ham sandwich and two custard cakes.

e Miguel wants a black coffee, one cod cake and one custard cake.

Listen to and read the dialogue on the next page, with reference to this menu.

PREPARAMOS ANIVERSÁRIOS   RUA BRAAMCAMP, 62

BANNER'S

COMIDA RÁPIDA DE LISBOA – SOC. GESTÃO, LDA.
CONTRIBUINTE N. 502 367 857
RESTAURANTE 2 CLASSE

SEXTAS, SÁBADOS E VÉSPERAS
DE FERIADOS
ABERTO ATÉ 02 HORAS DA
MADRUGADA

ABERTO TODOS OS DIAS
DAS 11.30H ÀS 24.00H

PIZZAS

1	MARGARITA	Molho de tomate, queijo, oregão
2	FANTASIA	Salame
3	ROMANA	Anchovas, ovo, fiambre
4	VEGETARIANA	Pimentos verdes, cogumelos, cebola
5	RAINHA	Fiambre, cogumelos, tomate
6	MAFIOSO	Salame, pimentos verdes, cebola
7	EXÓTICA	Ananás, fiambre
8	QUATRO ESTAÇÕES	Salame, fiambre, cogumelos, azeitonas, ovo
9	NEPTUNO	Camarão, mexilhão, berbigão, azeitonas
10	FRANGO	Frango, cogumelos, azeitonas
11	MEXICALE	Feijão, piri piri, tomate, alface, carne picada
12	BANNER'S	Salame, cogumelos, pimentos verdes, fiambre, pepperoni, cebola
13	CALZONE	Qualquer Pizza (de cima), fechada

▶ Diálogo

Nuno e Miguel estão com pressa e querem comer alguma coisa rápida.

Nuno and Miguel are in a rush and want to eat some fast food.

Nuno　　Então, o que vais escolher?

Miguel　Bom, para mim, acho que quero uma pizza Romana, com uma dose de batatas fritas.

Nuno　　Tens muita fome! Eu só quero uma pizza Frango, e mais nada.

Miguel　Não bebes nada?

Nuno　　Vou pedir uma Pepsi. E tu, o que queres?

Miguel　Pois, eu também quero um refrigerante. Talvez uma 7 Up.

Nuno　　Está bem, então vamos pedir, senão, vamos chegar atrasados ao cinema.

Empregada　Façam favor?

Miguel　É uma pizza Romana com batatas fritas, uma pizza Frango, uma Pepsi e uma 7-Up, se faz favor.

Empregada　É para levar, ou vão comer aqui dentro?

Miguel　É para comer aqui. Obrigado.

acho que	*I think that*
uma dose	*a portion*
fome	*hunger*
e mais nada	*and nothing else*
um refrigerante	*soft drink*
pedir	*to ask for / order*
para levar	*to take out / away*

Exercises

2　Look at the menu for Banner's pizzeria on page 134. Which pizzas would you ask for if you wanted the following toppings?

　a　chicken / mushrooms / olives
　b　pineapple / ham
　c　a pizza with lettuce on it
　d　one with egg and mushrooms
　e　one with shrimps

3　**a**　When is Banner's open?
　b　At what times?
　c　When is 'student night'?

d   Ask your friend what they're having.
e   Say that you think you'll have a chicken pizza.
f   Tell your friend he / she is hungry.
g   Ask your friend if they're not drinking anything.
h   Say you'll ask for a lemonade (7-Up).
i   Ask your friend if they want a soft drink.
j   Say you want a portion of chips.

i Eating and drinking out

There are plenty of places in Portugal where you can eat and drink. If you just want a snack, go to a café or café-bar or **pastelaria** (where cakes abound). For main meals you could choose a **restaurante**; some of these are graded by a 'star' system, others have their own fame, or there are the **tascas** – usually more reasonably priced and, up to recently, only frequented by men – here you can buy drink straight from the barrel. It's worth asking around to find a **tasca** with a good reputation. Other eating places may have obscure names and you'll only find them by talking to locals.

i Drinks

Beer (**cerveja**) is really like the lager drunk in the UK, or American beer, and if you are accustomed to imported lager such as the Spanish San Miguel, Portuguese beers such as Sagres and Superbock are very similar. Ask for **uma imperial** for draught Portuguese beer and **uma caneca** for a pint glass. Wine is the thing to drink in Portugal, as it is cheap and, in the main, of excellent quality.

vinho branco	white wine
vinho tinto	red
vinho verde	'green' wine
vinho verde tinto	red 'green' wine (young and fruity)
vinho rosé	rosé
vinho do Porto	port wine

▶ 3   Listen to the recording and look at your snacks and drinks Bingo card. When you hear your items called out in Portuguese, cross them off. You will be left with one item – can you say what it is in Portuguese?

Milky coffee	Custard cake
Red wine	Chips
Orange juice	Cheese sandwich

Documento

What drinks did these people have with their meal?

RESTAURANTE ℱloresta
CAFÉ
CERVEJARIA da Cidade

Contribuinte n.º 805 595 570

Travessa Poço da Cidade, 10-12 – 1200 Lisboa
Telef. 346 06 21

TALÃO DE MESA

Couvert	€ 3,25
Aperitivos	2,70
Sopa	
Peixe	
Carne	13,20
Marisco	
Pão	1,00
Vinho	6,45
Águas	1,40
Refrigerantes	
Cerveja	

▶ Leitura *Reading*

A comida portuguesa *Portuguese food*

See how much of this you understand. Listen to it on the recording a few times.

A comida portuguesa é muito variada e deliciosa. Cada região tem os seus próprios pratos típicos como, por exemplo, as tripas no Porto; a carne de porco à Alentejana, no Alentejo; e em Trás-os-Montes, a feijoada. Os portugueses comem muito peixe, como as sardinhas (assadas), e o bacalhau – dizem que existem 365 receitas para o bacalhau, uma para cada dia do ano! Os mariscos comem-se bastante, em pratos como arroz de marisco, e açorda de marisco. As sopas portuguesas são realmente uma delícia, espessas e muito saudáveis. Experimente o caldo verde. Há sempre pão com as refeições, caseiro, e muito bom. Usa-se muito alho e azeite na cozinha portuguesa, e muito sal – e é por isso que é aconselhável beber bastante água. Os portugueses adoram doces e sobremesas como pudim flan, mousse de chocolate, e gelados.

a comida	*food, cuisine*
cada	*each*
os seus próprios	*their own*
as tripas	*tripe*
a carne de porco à Alentejana	*pork and clams*
a feijoada	*bean and pork stew*
sardinhas assadas	*grilled sardines*
o bacalhau	*salted cod*
os mariscos	*seafood*
arroz de marisco	*seafood rice*
açorda de marisco	*seafood / bread mixture*
espessas e muito saudáveis	*thick and very healthy*
o caldo verde	*shredded kale soup*
as refeições	*meals*
pão-caseiro	*home-made bread*
alho	*garlic*
azeite	*olive oil*
é aconselhável	*it's advisable*
sobremesas	*desserts*
pudim flan	*crême caramel*
gelados	*ice creams*

A ementa / a lista *The menu*

<table>
<tr><td colspan="2">a ementa / a lista</td></tr>
<tr><td>Entradas</td><td>Starters</td></tr>
<tr><td>Carnes</td><td>Meat</td></tr>
<tr><td>Peixes</td><td>Fish</td></tr>
<tr><td>Sobremesas / Doces</td><td>Sweets</td></tr>
<tr><td>Bebidas</td><td>Drinks</td></tr>
<tr><td>Vinhos</td><td>Wines</td></tr>
<tr><td>Couvert</td><td>Cover charge</td></tr>
</table>

<table>
<tr><td colspan="2">pratos do dia</td></tr>
<tr><td></td><td>€</td></tr>
<tr><td>costeletas de porco</td><td>5,40</td></tr>
<tr><td>escalopes de peru</td><td>5,90</td></tr>
<tr><td>bacalhau à Gomes Sá</td><td>6,20</td></tr>
<tr><td>arroz de marisco</td><td>9,70/4,60</td></tr>
<tr><td>laranja</td><td>0,70</td></tr>
<tr><td>mousse</td><td>1,50</td></tr>
<tr><td>pudim</td><td>1,60</td></tr>
</table>

ℹ Menus

Your main menu is divided up as in the first **ementa** above. **Couvert** is a cover charge for bread, butter, and so on. Be careful in some restaurants, especially the more tourist-orientated ones: your table will be laden with plates of olives, cheese, ham, shrimps. These are a real temptation to nibble on, and a pricey one at that. The products are sometimes expensive, and if you should decide to bite into just one shrimp, eat just one olive, you will be charged for the plateful! The best thing to do is to establish from the outset exactly what you want, and ask them to take the other plates away.

ℹ Pratos do dia *Dishes of the day*

On the board above, you have been given a choice of pork chops, turkey steaks, bacalhau, or seafood rice. These will usually be served with salad, rice and chips. You will see some dishes have a cheaper price for a **meia dose** = half portion. As Portuguese portions are generally huge, this is an option worth considering. For dessert you have been offered oranges, mousse or crême caramel.

ℹ Ementa turística *Tourist (set) menu*

This is usually of average value, but offers a complete meal, with drinks, and means you don't have to spend time on lengthy deliberations.

> *A ementa turística*
> *Pão e manteiga*
> *carne de porco*
> *ou*
> *pescada*
> *mousse de chocolate*
> *ou*
> *salada de frutas*
> *½ garrafa de vinho /*
> *refrigerante*
> *café*
> *€ 8,40*

The menu above gives:

bread and butter
pork or hake
chocolate mousse or fruit salad
½ bottle wine / soft drink
coffee

Exercises

▶ 4   **Actividade quatro:** Fill in your part of the conversation with the waiter.

	Empregado	Boa noite. Faz favor.
a	**You**	*Greet the waiter and ask if there is any soup.*
	Empregado	Sim, hoje temos sopa de marisco ou caldo verde.
b	**You**	*Say you'd like a caldo verde.*
	Empregado	E depois, para comer?
c	**You**	*Tell him you'd like a half portion of the cod dish. Ask him if there is salad with it.*
	Empregado	Sim, vem com uma pequena salada mista.
d	**You**	*Say that's OK.*
	Empregado	E para sobremesa?

e	You	Say you'll have the crême caramel.

Empregado E para beber?

f	You	Tell him you'll have half a bottle of white wine and a black coffee afterwards.

e **You** *Say you'll have the crême caramel.*

Empregado E para beber?

f **You** *Tell him you'll have half a bottle of white wine and a black coffee afterwards.*

5 An inattentive waiter has set out this menu incorrectly. Where should each item appear?

EMENTA

1 carne de porco à Alentejana
2 açorda de marisco
3 pão   A) Entradas
4 vinho da casa
5 queijo da Serra
6 manteiga   B) Carnes
7 salada de frutas
8 café
9 pudim Molotov   C) Peixes
10 sopa de legumes
11 refrigerantes
12 bolo de chocolate   D) Sobremesas
13 caldo verde
14 prato de camarão
15 bacalhau à Brás   E) Bebidas
16 escalopes de peru
17 cerveja – imperial
18 pescada
19 mousse de chocolate   F) Couvert
20 água mineral

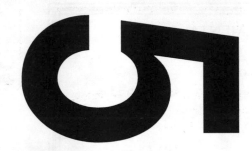

15

feeling ill

sentir-se mal

In this unit you will learn
- how to talk about minor ailments and remedies
- how to discuss illness
- how to cope with accidents and hospitals
- how to deal with the chemist and doctor

Before you begin

If you do have the misfortune to fall ill while in Portugal, and your ailment is only minor, you should go to the chemist's (**a farmácia**). Portuguese pharmacists are usually extremely helpful, and will give advice on any problem so that you may not need to go to see a doctor (**um médico**). Consultations have to be paid for. You may go to a local health centre (**centro de saúde**) or the hospital (**o hospital**) if the problem is serious. Treatment at the dentist (**o dentista**) is expensive.

Grammar

Be prepared for dealing with medical problems by learning some of the following basic language. In general, if a part of the body hurts, you say: **dói-me** (or **doem-me** in the plural), plus the part of the body that hurts.

Dói-me a cabeça.	*My head hurts.*
Doem-me os dentes.	*My teeth hurt.*

You can also say: **Tenho uma dor de** + part of the body.

Tenho uma dor de garganta. *I have a sore throat.*

If you are reporting on someone else's problem, the expressions become:

Dói-lhe . . .	*His / her . . . hurts.*
Doem-lhe . . .	*His / her . . . hurt.*

And:

(Ele) tem . . .	*(He) has . . .*
(Ela) tem . . .	*(She) has . . .*

In these circumstances you might well need the names of family members, if you want to say *my husband, son,* etc. and so on. Why not revise Unit 4 now so that you're prepared for the exercises in this unit?

Look at the body (**o corpo**) on the next page for other parts of the body, and note that you do not say *my* head hurts, but simply *the* head hurts. For sore ears you say **doem-me os ouvidos**, and not **orelhas** (**orelha** is the outer ear).

▶ Listen to the recording, and as each part of the body is said, identify it on the diagram, then repeat the word.

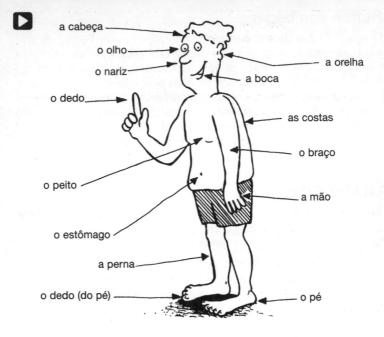

- a cabeça
- o olho
- o nariz
- o dedo
- o peito
- o estômago
- a perna
- o dedo (do pé)
- a orelha
- a boca
- as costas
- o braço
- a mão
- o pé

Other problems you might need to report include:

estou constipado/a	*I have a cold*
tenho gripe	*I have flu*
tenho uma insolação	*I have sunstroke*
tenho uma enxaqueca	*I have a migraine*
cortei (cortou) . . .	*I've (he's, she's) cut . . .*
bati (bateu) . . .	*I've (he's, she's) banged . . .*
magoei (magoou) . . .	*I've (he's, she's) hurt . . .*

▶ Diálogo

Maria isn't feeling very well.

João Olá, Maria, estás bem?

Maria Não, não estou. Tenho uma dor de cabeça.

João Tomaste um remédio?

Maria Sim, tomei uma aspirina há meia hora.

João Então, porque não te vais deitar um pouquinho – vais sentir-te melhor depois.

Maria Tens razão. Vou já para casa.

tomaste . . . ?	*have you taken . . . ?*
um remédio	*medicine*
tomei	*I've taken (I took)*
tens razão	*you're right*
há meia hora	*1/2 hr ago*
porque não te vais deitar	*why don't you go and lie down*
um pouquinho	*a little bit*
sentir-te	*to feel*
vou já	*I'm going right now*

▶ Diálogo

Mr Carvalho feels ill.

Ana	Bom dia, senhor Carvalho. Como está?
Sr Carvalho	Não me sinto bem.
Ana	Qual é o problema?
Sr Carvalho	Sinto-me tonto e creio que vou vomitar.
Ana	Não era melhor sentar-se um pouco?
Sr Carvalho	Boa ideia. Vou ficar aqui uns momentos.

não me sinto bem	*I don't feel well*
o problema	*problem*
sinto-me tonto	*I feel dizzy*
creio que	*I think that*
vomitar	*to be sick*
não era melhor . . . ?	*wouldn't it be better . . . ?*
sentar-se	*to sit down*

Exercise

1 How would you say the following?

a I have a sore throat.
b My daughter has cut her finger.
c My ears hurt.
d My husband has sunstroke.
e I think my son is going to be sick.
f I've banged my toe.
g My friend has hurt her leg.

ℹ️ If you are involved in, or need to report, an accident in Portugal, the following information is vital:

Telephone number 112 gets through to the emergency services.

Houve um acidente.	*There's been an accident.*
Precisamos duma ambulância.	*We need an ambulance.*
Precisamos de ajuda.	*We need help.*

Be prepared to give details:

onde?	*where?*	**o seu nome?**	*your name?*
pessoas feridas?	*injured people?*		

Speaking on the phone is a daunting task, especially in a situation like this, so try to keep calm, and don't forget useful phrases like:

Por favor fale mais devagar.	*Please speak more slowly.*
Pode repetir?	*Can you repeat?*
Sou inglês / inglesa.	*I am English.*

O hospital in Portugal can be a bewildering experience. You will be looked after, but be prepared for some form-filling. Provided you take your passport and/or the European Health card, you will be charged the minimum tax for access to the service (around 9 euros).

Exercise

2   Would you know how to fill in a form (**uma ficha**) like the one below? See how much you can do before looking at the word box. In practice, you will simply be asked for most of the relevant details.

```
┌─────────────────────────────────────────────────────────────┐
│         FICHA DE DADOS PESSOAIS – Centro de Saúde            │
│  NOME COMPLETO _____          │
│  IDADE _____        │
│  DATA DE NASCIMENTO _____          │
│  LUGAR DE NASCIMENTO _____          │
│  MORADA _____          │
│  NÚMERO DE TELEFONE/TELEMÓVEL _____           │
│  BILHETE DE IDENTIDADE _____          │
│  NÚMERO DE CONTRIBUINTE _____           │
│  EM CASO DE EMERGÊNCIA CONTACTAR –                          │
└─────────────────────────────────────────────────────────────┘
```

nome completo	full name
idade	age
data de nascimento	date of birth
lugar de nascimento	place of birth
morada	address
número de telefone/telemóvel	telephone/mobile number
bilhete de identidade	identity card number (or passport for tourists)
número de contribuinte	national insurance number (put personal insurance details if known)
em caso de emergência, contactar . . .	in case of emergency, contact . . .

▶ Diálogo

Na farmácia *At the chemist's*

Senhora	Tem alguma coisa para dor de garganta?
Farmacêutico	É para si, ou para uma criança?
Senhora	Para mim.
Farmacêutico	Só tem dor de garganta, ou tem outros sintomas também?
Senhora	Tenho uma dorzinha de cabeça também.
Farmacêutico	Bom. Recomendo este xarope para a garganta – tome três vezes por dia. E para a cabeça, estes comprimidos, ou estas aspirinas.
Senhora	Levo os comprimidos.
Farmacêutico	Tome dois de seis em seis horas.

tem alguma coisa para . . . ?	*do you have something for . . .?*
para si, mim	*for you, me*
criança	*child*
sintomas	*symptoms*
recomendo	*I recommend*
xarope	*syrup / cough mixture*
três vezes por dia	*three times a day*
ou	*or*
comprimidos	*pills*
levo	*I'll take*
de seis em seis horas	*every six hours*

Documento

For what part of the body is this medicine being advertised?

**Quando
a garganta
arde
e queima...**

para alívio rápido

... a solução é Calmacaína.

Grammar

Remédios *Medicines*

The following vocabulary might be useful:

comprimidos	*pills*
aspirina ⎫	many medicines
paracetemol ⎬	are known by their
migraleve ⎭	brand name
uma ligadura	*bandage*
um band-aid / um penso rápido	*plaster*
creme para . . .	*cream for . . .*
loção para . . .	*lotion for . . .*

Leitura *Reading*

Look at the information below on health and emergency contacts, and see if you can answer the questions below.

1 What number would you ring if you needed a doctor urgently?
2 On the Lisbon pharmacy phone lines, for what do you have to pay 1.85 euros?
3 What do you get if you dial 112?
4 In Viseu, which number would you ring if you wanted the district hospital?
5 Why might you ring 26216?

FARMÁCIAS

LISBOA

Das 22 às 9 horas, chamadas com receitas do dia ou da véspera – €0,30. Chamadas não urgentes – €1,85.

MÉDICO DE URGÊNCIA
☎ 796 06 90

NÚMERO NACIONAL DE SOCORRO

112

VISEU (032)
Bombeiros Municipais – 26216
Bombeiros Voluntários – 26812
Hospital Distrital – 424124
GNR – 421958 e 421585
Brigada de Trânsito – 26637
PSP – 422041
Aeródromo de Viseu – 459849
Electricidade
(Falta de luz e água) – 425175
Serviços Municipalizados – 423112
Rodoviária Beira Litoral – 422822

Exercise

▶ 3 Listen to five people on the recording saying what is wrong with them, and decide if the following statements are True or False.

1 His leg hurts   T/F
2 She has a sore throat   T/F
3 His teeth hurt   T/F
4 She has sunstroke   T/F
5 He's cut his arm   T/F

16 viajar de carro
travelling by car

In this unit you will learn
- how to deal with cars and travel documents
- how to cope with petrol and service stations
- information on roads and road signs
- how to report accidents and theft

Before you begin

Driving in Portugal can be somewhat daunting, even for the most experienced of drivers: many roads are awkward to handle, owing to bad surfaces and pot holes. Portuguese drivers are notoriously difficult to deal with, and driving rules and regulations are constantly changing. If you hire a car, make sure you always travel with the appropriate documentation, such as current driving licence, insurance, proof of hire and, if you borrow a vehicle from friends, you must have a letter of authorization to drive it.

▶ Diálogo

Listen to, then read, the following dialogue.

Miguel pede informações sobre o caminho para a Nazaré.
Michael asks for information about the way to Nazaré.

Miguel   Desculpe, é este o caminho certo para a Nazaré?

Senhora   Ah, não é exactamente, não. Era melhor seguir por esta estrada até à rotunda, e ali tomar a segunda saída, e seguir por aquele caminho.

Miguel   Vai demorar muito?

Senhora   Acho que não. A Nazaré fica a oitenta quilómetros daqui, mais ou menos. Se seguir a estrada A1, vai logo ver os sinais para a Nazaré. É um instantinho.

Miguel   Muito obrigado e bom dia.

o caminho certo	*the right way*
exactamente	*exactly*
era melhor	*it would be better*
a estrada	*road, highway*
a rotunda	*roundabout*
a saída	*exit*
Vai demorar muito?	*Is it going to take a long time?*
A Nazaré fica a 80 quilómetros daqui.	*Nazaré is 80 km away.*
Acho que não.	*I don't think so.*
mais ou menos	*more or less*
se seguir	*if you follow*
a estrada A1	*national highway A1*
vai logo ver	*you'll soon see*
os sinais	*road signs*
é um instantinho	*it's really quick*

Grammar

Study the diagram of a car (**o carro / o automóvel**), and try to learn the names of the various parts. You never know what might make you break down at any time when you are travelling!

o pára-brisas
o retrovisor
o volante
o porta-bagagens
a capota
o motor
o depósito
a roda
a porta
a matrícula
o pneu
o limpa-pára-brisas

▶ Diálogo

Manuela telefona para uma garagem para pedir ajuda. *Manuela telephones a (repair) garage to ask for help.*

Mecánico Oficina Oliveira, boa tarde.

Manuela Boa tarde. Faz favor, preciso de ajuda.

Mecánico Qual é o problema?

Manuela O meu carro está avariado. Creio que há um furo num pneu, er mas também tive problemas com os travões.

Mecánico Onde está o carro?

Manuela Estou na EN 125, perto de Loulé, ao lado duma escola.

Mecánico Bom, então espere dentro do carro, vou organizar um reboque.

Manuela Vai demorar?

Mecánico Pode demorar um pouco porque não conheço bem o caminho.

Manuela Paciência!

avariado	broken down
creio que	I think, believe that
um furo	puncture
tive problemas	I've had (some) problems
os travões	brakes
a EN 125 (= Estrada Nacional)	the 125 highway
uma escola	school
espere	wait
organizar	organize
um reboque	lift, tow
não conheço bem	I don't know well
paciência!	patience! (Be patient!)

Grammar

Conhecer, saber To know

There are two verbs in Portuguese that mean *to know* (you met them previously in Unit 9). You'll no doubt remember that **conhecer** means to know a person or place, and **saber** means to know a fact. Here are the two verbs in full in the present tense.

	conhecer	saber
Eu	conheço	sei
Tu	conheces	sabes
Ele, ela você o Sr/a Sra	conhece	sabe
nós	conhecemos	sabemos
eles, elas vocês os Srs	conhecem	sabem

Exercise

1 Decide which of the two verbs (**saber / conhecer**) should go in each sentence. The correct form is provided in the brackets to help you.

a A Maria ___ o meu irmão. [sabe / conhece]
b Nós não ___ as horas. [sabemos / conhecemos]

c   Tu queres ___ a França?   [conhecer / saber]
d   Eles ___ o Presidente.   [sabem / conhecem]
e   O João não ___ o meu nome.   [conhece / sabe]

▶ Diálogo

O senhor Neto quer comprar gasolina. *Mr Neto wants to buy some petrol.*

Senhor Neto	Boa tarde. Quero gasolina, se faz favor.
Attendant	Claro. Quer sem chumbo ou gasóleo?
Senhor Neto	Sem chumbo.
Attendant	Quantos litros?
Senhor Neto	Pode encher o depósito. Preciso também de pôr ar nos pneus, e quero dois litros de óleo, por favor.
Attendant	Muito bem.
Senhor Neto	Aceita cartões de crédito?
Attendant	Aceitamos, sim.

gasolina	*petrol*
sem chumbo	*unleaded petrol*
gasóleo, óleo	*diesel, oil*
quantos litros?	*how many litres?*
pode encher o depósito	*you can fill the tank*
pôr	*to put*
ar	*air*
aceita / aceitamos	*(you) accept / we accept*
cartões de crédito	*credit cards*

Exercise

2   See how many of the following you can do.

a   Ask if this is the correct way to Lisbon.
b   Ask if it's going to take a long time.
c   Say that your car is broken down.
d   Say that you need a tow.
e   Say that you want eight litres of unleaded petrol.
f   Ask if someone accepts credit cards.
g   Tell someone to fill the tank up.

Leitura *Reading*

Read the following passage on driving regulations in Portugal, and see how much of it you can understand.

Conduzir em Portugal: Umas regras gerais

- É obrigatório usar cintos de segurança; crianças menores de 12 anos devem viajar no banco traseiro.

- O limite aceitável (e legal) de álcool é de menos de 0.4 gramas por litro. Apesar da grande campanha contra 'o beber' e 'o conduzir' ('Bebeu? Não conduza!'), é surpreendente quantas pessoas continuam a sair para tomar uns copos, e voltar para casa de carro.

- Todos os veículos devem ter uma caixa de Pronto-Socorros, e um triângulo vermelho para montar na estrada no caso de avaria.

- Os limites de velocidade – 50 quilómetros por hora dentro de cidades / 90 q.p.h. nas estradas / 120 q.p.h. nas auto-estradas. Para veículos maiores, tais como camiões e camionetas, os limites chegam a ser aproximadamente 20 por cento mais baixos.

- Se há menos de um ano que se conduz, deve-se observar um limite de velocidade de 90 quilómetros por hora, e deve-se expor um autocolante no vidro traseiro do carro.

cintos de segurança	*safety-belts*
deve / devem / deve-se	*must*
banco traseiro	*back seat*
o limite aceitável	*acceptable limit*
apesar de	*in spite of*
conduzir	*driving, to drive*
Bebeu? Não conduza!	*Have you had a drink? Don't drive!*
surpreendente	*surprising*
tomar uns copos	*to have a few drinks*
uma caixa de Pronto-Socorros	*first-aid box*
montar	*to erect*
no caso de	*in the event of*
avaria	*break-down*

tais como	such as
camiões e camionetas	lorries and coaches
chegam a ser	come to be / are
mais baixos	lower
há menos de um ano	it's less than a year
um autocolante	a (special) sticker
o vidro traseiro	back window

Exercise

3 Can you answer these questions in Portuguese?

a É obrigatório usar cintos de segurança?
b Todos os veículos devem ter o quê?
c É legal beber e conduzir em Portugal?
d Se há menos de um ano que se conduz, o que deve fazer?
e Qual é o limite de velocidade para carros nas auto-estradas?

i If you are involved in a traffic accident, follow the instructions for getting help In Unit 15. You will also need to fill in all kinds of forms, and give a statement to the traffic police (usually the GNR – Guarda Nacional Republicana, or brigada do Trânsito).

If you experience theft from your vehicle, you will need to report it at the local **Esquadra da Polícia** (police station). Dealing with the police in Portugal can be difficult: if you can find someone to go with you, it will certainly help.

▶ Diálogo

A senhora Johnson informa a Polícia sobre um roubo. *Mrs Johnson reports a theft to the police.*

Senhora Johnson	Bom dia. Chamo-me Sylvia Johnson e sou inglesa. Estou aqui de férias. Quero comunicar o roubo dalgumas coisas no meu carro.
Polícia	Que coisas?
Senhora Johnson	A minha máquina fotográfica, o meu telemóvel, e uma mala que continha o meu passaporte e carteira com dinheiro.
Polícia	Como aconteceu?

Senhora Johnson	O vidro está partido.
Polícia	A senhora não sabe que corre um grande risco, deixar objectos dentro do carro?
Senhora Johnson	Eu sei, mas só demorei um pouco.
Polícia	Vai ter de preencher esta ficha em triplicado. Tem os seus documentos?

comunicar	*to report*
o roubo	*theft*
que coisas?	*which things?*
a máquina fotográfica	*camera*
uma mala que continha . . .	*a bag which contained . . .*
o passaporte	*passport*
a carteira	*purse, wallet*
dinheiro	*money*
como aconteceu?	*how did it happen?*
partido	*broken*
corre um grande risco	*you run a big risk*
deixar	*to leave / leaving*
objectos	*objects*
só demorei um pouco	*I was only a little while*
preencher	*to fill in*
ficha	*form*
em triplicado	*in triplicate*

Exercise

4   There are eight words connected with cars hidden in this wordsearch. Can you find them?

P	N	E	U	F	V	S	Q	S	G
F	E	U	Q	P	B	E	R	E	A
O	U	N	J	K	W	A	E	O	S
T	C	B	Y	I	D	V	P	V	O
I	B	M	L	A	W	A	P	A	L
S	L	P	R	F	B	R	J	R	I
O	M	T	D	L	M	I	G	T	N
P	S	M	K	B	T	A	J	T	A
E	G	H	Q	A	P	D	C	X	W
D	M	K	Y	W	Q	O	E	L	O

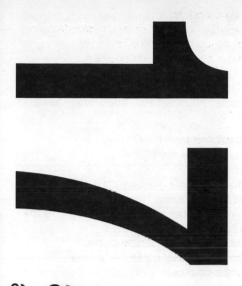

17 alojamento
accommodation

In this unit you will learn
- how to find lodgings
- how to book accommodation
- what to do when things don't work

Listen to, and read through, the following short dialogues relating to hotel accommodation.

Diálogos

▶ A família Santos procura quartos num hotel. *The Santos family look for rooms in a hotel.*

Senhor Santos Tem quartos vagos para hoje?
Recepcionista Temos, sim. Quantos são?
Senhor Santos Somos cinco.
Recepcionista É para quantas noites?
Senhor Santos Vamos ficar cinco noites.
Recepcionista Querem um quarto de família ou quartos individuais?
Senhor Santos O quarto de família tem quantas camas?
Recepcionista Tem uma cama de casal e três camas individuais.
Senhor Santos Então, ficamos com este.

tem quartos vagos?	*do you have any rooms free?*
quantos são?	*how many of you are there?*
somos cinco	*there are five of us*
para quantas noites?	*for how many nights?*
ficar	*to stay*
um quarto de família	*a family room*
quartos individuais	*single rooms*
cama de casal	*double bed*
camas individuais	*single beds*
ficamos com este	*we'll have this one*

▶ Sônia encontra um problema. *Sônia comes across a problem.*

Sônia Tem quartos vagos?
Recepcionista Para quantas pessoas?
Sônia Só para uma.
Recepcionista Para quando?
Sônia Para hoje e amanhã.
Recepcionista Lamento, mas já não há quartos individuais para hoje. Talvez haja no hotel Sol, que fica aqui em frente.
Sônia Está bem. Obrigada pela ajuda.

para quantas pessoas?	*for how many people?*
para quando?	*for when?*
lamento	*I'm sorry*
já não há	*there are no longer*
talvez haja	*perhaps there may be*
obrigada pela ajuda	*thanks for the help*

▶ A senhora Jones quer reservar um quarto. *Mrs Jones wants to book a room. She telephones the Lusa guest house.*

Senhora Jones	Está?
Recepcionista	Estou, sim.
Senhora Jones	É da pensão Lusa?
Recepcionista	É sim. Bom dia.
Senhora Jones	Olá bom dia. Queria reservar um quarto de casal para o dia 22.
Recepcionista	Quantas noites pretendem ficar?
Senhora Jones	Três.
Recepcionista	Quer com casa de banho privativa?
Senhora Jones	Sim, se faz favor, e pequeno almoço.
Recepcionista	Qual é o nome?
Senhora Jones	É Jones.
Recepcionista	Como se escreve?
Senhora Jones	J–O–N–E–S.
Recepcionista	Muito bem, senhora Jones. Está reservado. Até ao dia 22. Bom dia, com licença.

está?	*hello (on the phone – lit are you?)*
estou	*hello (on the phone – lit I am)*
a pensão	*guest house*
reservar	*to reserve*
um quarto de casal	*a double room*
pretendem	*you (pl) intend, want*
casa de banho privativa	*en-suite bathroom*
como se escreve?	*how do you write it?*
reservado	*reserved*
com licença	*excuse me (to end phone conversation)*

Exercise

1 How would you do the following:

a Ask if there are rooms free?
b Say there are three of you?
c Say you'd like to reserve a single room?
d Ask if that's the Pensão Sol?
e Ask how much it is with breakfast?

Grammar

Hotel talk

um quarto	*a room*
um quarto individual / simples	*single room*
um quarto duplo	*double / twin room*
um quarto de casal	*double room*
um quarto de família	*a family room*
com cama de casal	*with double bed*
com duas camas	*with twin beds*
com cama de criança	*with a child's bed*

10° DÉCIMO
9° NONO
8° OITAVO
7° SÉTIMO
6° SEXTO
5° QUINTO
4° QUARTO
3° TERCEIRO
2° SEGUNDO
1° PRIMEIRO
R/C (res-do-chão)

▶ Diálogo

O Sr Green tem um quarto reservado. *Mr Green has a room booked.*

Senhor Green	Boa noite. Tenho um quarto reservado para hoje e amanhã.
Recepcionista	Em que nome?
Senhor Green	Green. G–R–E–E–N
Recepcionista	Aqui está, senhor Green. É o quarto trezentos e vinte e cinco. Fica no terceiro andar; o elevador é ali à direita.
Senhor Green	Tem uma vista bonita?
Recepcionista	Tem, sim. O quarto dá para o mar. Faça favor de preencher esta ficha. Preciso de ficar com o seu passaporte.

o elevador	*lift*
uma vista bonita	*a lovely view*
o quarto dá para o mar	*the room overlooks the sea*
faça favor de ...	*please ... (+ verb)*
preencher	*to fill in*
ficha	*form*
preciso de	*I need*
ficar com	*to keep*
o passaporte	*passport*

Documento

a How many people was this room for?
b How much extra was breakfast?

Hotel Miraparque

Quarto	311	Preço	€ 36
N.º Pessoas	2	Preço P. Almoço	GRÁTIS
Chegada	3/10/08	Partida	11/10/08
Nome	A. Hills		

Este cartão servirá para a identificação junto dos serviços do Hotel, que poderão exigir a sua apresentação; conserve este cartão para utilizar no caso de reclamação perante os Serviços Oficiais de Turismo.

AV. SIDÓNIO PAIS, 12 - LISBOA - PORTUGAL - TEL. 57 80 70 - FAX 57 89 20 - TELEX 16745 - MITEL P

ℹ️ There is a variety of accommodation available in Portugal, serving the needs and budget of everybody. You could stay in a **pousada de juventude** (*youth hostel*) if you are on a budget, or for a bit extra, try a **pensão** or **residencial** (*guest house*), where you can usually just get bed and breakfast.

Hotels, like everywhere, range from one to five stars. There is also the **estalagem** or **albergue** (*inn*), and for those who want to splash out a little bit more, the now privatized system of **pousadas** – converted castles, monasteries, and stately homes. Wherever you go, you will receive the famous Portuguese welcome.

▶ Diálogo

Quando as coisas não funcionam . . . *When things don't work . . .*

Laura	Desculpe, o aquecimento no quarto não está a funcionar bem.
Recepcionista	Qual é o número do quarto?
Laura	É o duzentos e quinze. É possível mandar alguém vir dar uma vista de olhos?
Recepcionista	Claro. Peço desculpa. Hoje temos tido alguns problemas. Como vê, o ascensor também está avariado. Creio que é por causa do corte de electricidade que tivemos ontem à noite. Vou ver se podemos arranjar qualquer coisa, está bem?
Laura	Obrigada.

o aquecimento	*the heating*
funcionar	*to work*
não está a funcionar bem	*isn't working well*
mandar	*to send*
alguém	*someone*
dar uma vista de olhos	*to have a look*
peço desculpa	*I'm sorry*
temos tido	*we've been having*
como vê	*as you can see*
o ascensor	*lift*
por causa de	*because of*
o corte de electricidade	*power cut*
tivemos	*we had*
ontem à noite	*last night*
arranjar	*to arrange*

Grammar

More verb forms

- **Estar** in the present tense + **a** + verb, conveys an action that is continuous or on-going. You can use this construction with any verb:

estou a falar	*I am speaking (now)*
estamos a pensar	*we are thinking*

- The simple past tense of **ter** (*to have*) is as follows:

(eu)	tive	*I had, have had*
(tu)	tiveste	*you had, have had*
(ele, ela/você)	teve	*he / she/ it / you had, have had*
(nós)	tivemos	*we had / have had*
(eles, elas, vocês)	tiveram	*they / you had / have had*

Talking about actions in the past is fairly complex, and in this course you have only met a few examples.

- To talk about an action that has been happening on a regular, or recent, basis, you need the following structure: **ter** (present tense) + past participle of verb.

Past participles are formed as follows:

  -ar verbs: falar → fal**ado**
  -er verbs: comer → com**ido**
  -ir verbs: partir → part**ido**

Remember, there are many irregular verbs which you will pick up in your later studies.

Tenho comprado muitas coisas.	*I've been buying many things.*
O João tem visitado muitos museus.	*John has been visiting many museums.*

Exercise

2 Can you match up these statements about things that are not working properly?

i   O elevador está avariado.   a *The cooker doesn't work.*
ii A água não está a funcionar.   b *The lift has broken down.*
iii O fogão não funciona.   c *The lock isn't working well.*
iv A fechadura não está a   d *The water isn't working.*
    funcionar bem.   e *The air-conditioning has*
v   O ar condicionado está   *broken down.*
    avariado.

Leitura *Reading*

Read this text on Pousadas, just to get the gist of it, and try to answer the questions.

POUSADAS DE PORTUGAL

Situadas em locais de rara beleza, as Pousadas de Portugal oferecem ao visitante amigo trinta e dois destinos para descobrir as tradições e hábitos das gentes de Portugal.

Com reduzida capacidade de alojamento, permitem um acolhimento atento e um serviço personalizado. No campo gastronómico, as Pousadas desvendam-nos os segredos de uma arte milenária recriando o melhor da cozinha regional, acompanhada pelos mais genuínos vinhos portugueses.

Na tranquilidade das pousadas de Portugal, descobrirá a maneira de viver e o sentir das cidades e aldeias deste país, restituindo-lhe o sentido da arte e do prazer de viajar.

1   Where are the Pousadas situated?
2   How many different destinations are there to choose from?
3   What kind of service is offered?
4   What type of food is offered?
5   What does the tranquillity of the Pousadas offer the visitor?

Exercise

▶ 3   **Actividade três:** Can you complete your part of this dialogue in a hotel?

a   **You**   *Ask if they have rooms free for today.*
     Recepcionista Temos, sim. Quantos são?
b   **You**   *Say there are three of you.*
     Recepcionista É para quantas noites?
c   **You**   *Say you're going to stay two nights.*
     Recepcionista Querem quartos individuais?
d   **You**   *Say you would like one double room and one single room.*
     Recepcionista Querem com casa de banho privativa?
e   **You**   *Say, yes, please; what is the price?*

■ Now let's see how much of the alphabet you can remember. Look back to page 4 and re-listen to the introductory section if you need a quick re-cap first, then listen to your recording.

18

fazer campismo
camping

In this unit you will learn
- all about campsites in Portugal
- how to discuss the weather
- how to interpret weather forecasts

Before you begin

Camping and caravanning in Portugal is popular and cheap, and there are numerous campsites (**parques de campismo**) to choose from, all over the country. Overnight parking in unofficial places is frowned upon.

▶ Diálogo

Listen to, then read, the following extended dialogue a couple of times until the phrases become more familiar to you.

Senhor de Sousa	Olá, bom dia. Tem vagas?
Recepcionista	Temos algumas. Tem tendas, carro e caravana ou carro-cama?
Senhor de Sousa	Temos carro e atrelado com duas tendas.
Recepcionista	Bom, temos vários lugares, há um à esquerda debaixo das árvores, outro ao fundo do parque, que dá para o lago, e há dois aqui ao pé do parque infantil.
Senhor de Sousa	Qual recomenda?
Recepcionista	Pois, é difícil. Aqui, perto do parque infantil é sempre mais barulhento; ao fundo do parque é sossegado, mas um pouco isolado, e debaixo das árvores, pois não sei se vai chover hoje, e é uma maçada ter a chuva a pingar em cima das tendas.
Senhor de Sousa	Vamos para o fundo. Gostamos do sossego.
Recepcionista	Vão ficar quanto tempo?
Senhor de Sousa	Se calhar, oito dias. Há uma loja aqui no parque?
Recepcionista	Aqui ao lado da recepção. Vende tudo, desde mercearias e jornais até garrafas de gás, e coberturas impermeáveis. Abre das 7.30 da manhã até às 9 e quinze da noite. Também há um bar e um pequeno café.

vagas	*spaces*
tendas	*tents*
carro e caravana	*car and caravan*
carro-cama	*camper van*
atrelado	*trailer*
as árvores	*the trees*
o lago	*lake*
o parque infantil	*children's playground*

recomenda	(you) recommend
difícil	difficult
barulhento	noisy
sossegado	quiet
isolado	isolated
vai chover	it's going to rain
é uma maçada	it's a pain
a chuva	rain
pingar	to drip
o sossego	the quiet
se calhar (colloquial)	probably
a recepção	reception
vende	it sells
desde . . . até . . .	from . . . to . . .
mercearias	groceries
coberturas impermeáveis	ground sheets

Exercise

1 Can you answer these questions based on the dialogue?

   a Tem vagas no parque de campismo?
   b O senhor de Sousa tem caravana?
   c Como é a vista ao fundo do parque?
   d Porque é uma maçada debaixo das árvores?
   e Onde escolhe (*chooses*) o senhor?
   f Quanto tempo vão ficar?
   g A loja vende que tipo de coisas?
   h A que horas abre?

Documento

Can you match up the symbols to the names on this campsite list?

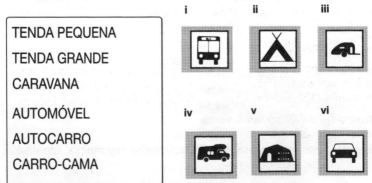

TENDA PEQUENA

TENDA GRANDE

CARAVANA

AUTOMÓVEL

AUTOCARRO

CARRO-CAMA

Grammar

O tempo *The weather*

	Hoje *Today*	Amanhã *Tomorrow*
	Faz sol / Há sol. *It's sunny.*	Vai fazer sol. *It's going to be sunny.*
	Faz calor. Está calor (*colloq*). Está quente. *It's hot.*	Vai fazer calor. Vai estar quente. *It's going to be hot.*
	Faz vento. Há muito vento. *It's windy.*	Vai fazer vento. Vai haver vento. *It's going to be windy.*
	Está a chover. *It's raining.*	Vai chover. *It's going to rain.*
	Faz frio. Está frio. *It's cold.*	Vai fazer frio. Vai estar frio. *It's going to be cold.*
	Está a nevar. Há neve. *It's snowing.*	Vai nevar. Vai haver neve. *It's going to snow.*

▶ Diálogos

Listen to the following two short dialogues on your recording, and / or read them. Campers are discussing the weather problems. Then answer the **Verdadeiro / Falso** exercise below.

Manuel Ai! Que horror!
Sofia O que há?
Manuel Estou completamente picado pelos mosquitos. Deve ser por causa do calor.

Sofia	Olhe aqui também, toda a roupa está cheia de areia. Deve ser o vento.
Manuel	Vamos procurar outro lugar.

Ai!	*Ahh!*
Que horror!	*Oh no / how awful!*
O que há?	*What's the matter? What's up?*
completamente	*completely*
picado	*stung / bitten*
os mosquitos	*mosquitoes*
deve ser	*it must be*
cheia de	*full of*
areia	*sand*

Luís	Ai! Não acredito!
Ana	O que há?
Luís	Temos um buraco. A água está a pingar dentro da tenda. Toda a roupa está molhada.
Ana	Olhe aqui também, a entrada está cheia de lama. Deve ser por causa da chuva.

não acredito	*I don't believe it*
um buraco	*leak, hole*
molhada	*wet*
lama	*mud*

Exercise

2   Say whether these statements, based on the two dialogues above, are **verdadeiro** (v) **ou falso** (f).

a   A Sofia está picada pelos mosquitos.
b   A roupa do Manuel está cheia de areia.
c   É por causa da chuva.
d   A tenda do Luís tem um buraco.
e   Há lama dentro da tenda.
f   É por causa da chuva.

Leitura *Reading*

Look at this weather picture, and see if you can correctly interpret the text. There is a vocabulary box on the next page.

Estado do tempo hoje às 16 horas

Hoje

No Continente:
Regiões do Norte e Centro: céu pouco nublado; vento fraco do quadrante leste; acentuado arrefecimento nocturno e formação de geada. *Estado do mar:* encrespado; ondulação noroeste de dois a três metros.

Regiões do Sul: céu pouco nublado, temporariamente muito nublado; vento fraco ou moderado de leste. *Estado do mar:* na costa ocidental, mar encrespado; ondulação noroeste de dois a três metros; na costa sul, mar encrespado ou de pequena vaga; ondulação sudeste de dois metros.

Amanhã

Céu geralmente limpo; vento fraco ou moderado de leste; acentuado arrefecimento nocturno com formação de geada.

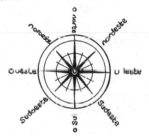

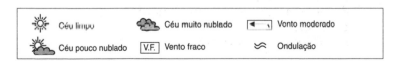

céu limpo	clear sky
céu pouco nublado	slightly cloudy sky
céu muito nublado	very cloudy sky
chuva	rain
trovoadas	thunder
nevoeiro	thick fog
vento fraco	light wind
neve	snow
vento moderado	moderate wind
geada	frost
vento forte	strong wind
ondulação	tides

Say whether these statements, based on the weather forecast on page 173, are **verdadeiro ou falso**.

1 Hoje no norte o vento está forte.
2 Amanhã em geral o céu vai estar limpo.
3 Hoje, perto de Beja, o vento está moderado.
4 Hoje, no sul, o mar tem uma ondulação de quatro metros.
5 Amanhã vai haver geada à noite.
6 Hoje, no centro, o vento é do sul.

Exercise

3 Match up these weather boxes with the appropriate captions.

i Faz frio.

a

ii Há neve.

b

iii Há sol.

c

iv Está a chover.

d

v Faz vento.

e

vi Há trovoadas.

f

4 Fill in the gaps on this table with weather expressions in the present or future tense using the *going to* construction.

Hoje	Amanhã
Faz calor.	**a** ___
Há sol.	**b** ___
c ___	Vai fazer frio.
Está a chover.	**d** ___
e ___	Vai haver vento.
f ___	Vai nevar.

▶ **5** Listen to the weather forecasts for four cities around the Portuguese-speaking world, and circle the correct word to complete each statement below. The answers are on the recording.

1 Today, in Lisbon, the wind is...
   a strong   **b** light

2 In Rio it's...
   a very hot   **b** warm

3 Tomorrow in Maputo the sky is going to be...
   a clear   **b** slightly cloudy

4 In Luanda it's going to...
   a be sunny   **b** rain

19 divertimentos

distractions

In this unit you will learn
- how to talk about activities on the beach
- how to talk about parks
- how to talk about cultural activities

▶ Diálogo

Jorge e Teresa decidem-se a ir à praia. *Jorge and Teresa decide to go to the beach.*

Jorge   Vamos à praia hoje?
Teresa Está bem. Faz calor, é ideal para ir nadar. Podemos levar um piquenique, e passar a tarde inteira. Que tal?
Jorge   Boa! Podemos jogar voleibol.
Teresa Tu podes jogar sozinho; eu quero apanhar o sol e dormir!
Jorge   Preguiçosa! Cuidado com o sol. É perigoso dormir. Precisamos de levar protecção contra o sol.

a praia	*beach*
é ideal para	*it's ideal for*
nadar	*to swim*
podemos	*we can*
levar	*to take*
um piquenique	*picnic*
a tarde inteira	*the whole afternoon*
que tal?	*what about (that)!*
boa! (*coll.*)	*great idea!*
voleibol	*volleyball*
sozinho	*alone*
apanhar o sol	*to sunbathe*
dormir	*to sleep*
preguiçosa	*lazy*
culdado	*careful*
é perigoso	*it's dangerous*
protecção	*protection*
oontra	*against*

▶ Diálogo

O Senhor Mendes e a Senhora Oliveira falam sobre o que fizeram ontem. *Mr Mendes and Mrs Oliveira talk about what they did yesterday.*

Senhor Mendes   O que fez ontem?
Senhora Oliveira Ontem, pois, fui com a minha família ao parque. Era um dia muito bonito para passear.
Senhor Mendes   O que fizeram lá?

Senhora Oliveira Levámos um piquenique, e andámos à sombra das árvores. Os meus filhos jogaram futebol, e vimos muitas coisas – pássaros, flores, e tantas borboletas!

Senhor Mendes Foram ao lago também?

Senhora Oliveira Fomos. Havia muita gente, portanto não conseguimos um barco, mas gostámos muito do passeio. E o senhor, fez alguma coisa interessante?

Senhor Mendes Eu? Trabalhei o dia inteiro!

o que fez ontem?	*what did you* (sing.) *do yesterday?*
fui / fomos / foram	*I went / we went / they, you went*
era	*it was*
o parque	*park*
passear	*to go for a stroll*
o que fizeram lá?	*what did you* (pl.) *do there?*
levámos	*we took*
andámos	*we walked*
à sombra das árvores	*in the shade of the trees*
jogaram	*(they) played*
vimos	*we saw*
pássaros, flores	*birds, flowers*
tantas	*so many*
borboletas	*butterflies*
o lago	*lake*
havia muita gente	*there were a lot of people*
não conseguimos	*we didn't manage (to get)*
gostámos	*we liked (enjoyed)*
trabalhei	*I worked*

Grammar

I came, I saw, I conquered

Talking in the past is a complex matter in Portuguese, and realistically falls outside the realms of this beginner's course. However, opposite you'll see the verb endings for the three regular verb groups, plus some irregular examples. These are for the simple past tense that you use when talking about completed actions.

	-ar fal/ar (to speak) [spoke]	-er com/er (to eat) [ate]	-ir part/ir (to leave) [left]
eu	FALei	COMi	PARTi
tu	FALaste	COMeste	PARTiste
ele, ela, você }	FALou	COMeu	PARTiu
nós	FALámos	COMemos	PARTimos
eles, elas vocês }	FALaram	COMeram	PARTiram
	ir (to go) [went]	fazer (to do, make) [did, made]	ver (to see) [saw]
eu	fui	fiz	vi
tu	foste	fizeste	viste
ele, ela, você }	foi	fez	viu
nós	fomos	fizemos	vimos
eles, elas vocês }	foram	fizeram	viram

Here are some common expressions that are useful when referring to past time.

ontem	yesterday
anteontem	the day before yesterday
a semana passada	last week
o mês passado	last month
o ano passado	last year
a quinta (feira) passada	last Thursday
nas férias passadas	last holiday
ontem à noite	last night

Exercises

1a Match up the people on the left, via a verb in the middle, to an activity on the right. In this way you'll be forming complete sentences in the past.

i	O Paulo	viste	ao parque.
ii	Tu	fizeram	o filme.
iii	Eu e a Maria	foi	ontem.
iv	Vocês	visitámos	muitas coisas interessantes.
v	Eu	trabalhei	a cidade.

1b Can you do the following?

i   Suggest that you and a friend go to the park today.
ii Say that you want to play football.
iii Ask your close friend what they did yesterday.
iv Say that you went to the beach.
v   Ask John if he liked the park.

i There are many things to see and do in Portugal. For example, you can visit some of the loveliest and oldest castles (**castelos**) and palaces (**palácios**) in Europe. There are many areas of outstanding natural beauty including parks, forests (**florestas**), and mountain ranges (**serras**). There are plenty of rich museums (**museus**), churches (**igrejas**) and art galleries (**galerias de arte**) to visit too.

You can participate in sport; tennis, golf, football, and water sports are popular, especially windsurfing. Or you can simply sit at an outdoor café, read a paper, sip a cooling drink, and watch the world go by.

Leitura *Reading*

You have been handed this leaflet about holiday activities in the Algarve. Read the description of the range of activities available to visitors. Just look for key words in each paragraph. You do not need to understand it all.

Região de turismo do Algarve

1

MERCADOS

Tudo se compra, tudo se vende. Desde a fresca hortaliça às flores perfumadas. E, também, fruta, objectos de uso diário, vestuário, etc.

2

EXPOSIÇÕES

Conhecer as obras de artistas portugueses e estrangeiros. Desvendar as tradições, o património cultural povo algarvio. Uma forma de enriquecer as suas férias.

3

FOLCLORE

A dança algarvia, é endiabrada, alegre, rápida. Fala de dias de sol, de corpos ágeis, de tradições que se revivem porque são eternas. E a sua música fica no ouvido...

4
DESPORTO

O sol sempre presente. Clima ameno nos 12 meses do ano. Variado e moderno equipamento. Razões que fazem do Algarve o paraíso dos desportistas.

5
PARQUES DE DIVERSÕES

A alegria e o sol juntam-se para horas de prazer, de puro divertimento. Uma forma sempre agradável de ver dias de férias com toda a família.

6
ACTIVIDADES CULTURAIS

Ciclo de passeios de natureza Alcalar e Senhora do Verde Passeio à descoberta do património natural e arqueológico desta zona do interior rural do concelho de Portimão.

7
FADO

Ouvir o fado é penetrar os segredos da alma portuguesa. Nos sons plangentes da guitarra, no canto que evoca amores e ciúmes, revela o sentido da palavra saudade. Fado é alegria e tristeza, é música que se ouve em silêncio, é uma recordação que fica para sempre.

Each member of your family likes different things. Look at the profiles of your family below for the purpose of this exercise, and decide which activity each member of the family would like the best. Match up the activity or sightseeing venue to the member of the family.

Your family profile

Mother	Likes looking at paintings. Wants to do something cultural, but prefers to be inside.
Father	Is keen on the outdoor life, and has an interest in old ruins, and areas of natural beauty.
Teenage brother	Wants to spend his time out in the sun playing tennis and windsurfing.
Two young sisters	Want to do an activity involving all the family.
Grandparents	Prefer something a bit less energetic. Grandad is an enthusiastic guitar player.

Exercise

▶ 2 **Actividade dois:** Complete the dialogue following the English prompts.

	Barbara	O que fez a semana passada?
a	**You**	*Say that last week you and your sister visited Lisbon.*
	Barbara	O que fizeram lá?
b	**You**	*Say that you went to a palace, and saw many interesting things.*
	Barbara	Levaram um piquenique?
c	**You**	*Say no, we ate in a café in the square.*
	Barbara	Gostaram da visita?
d	**You**	*Say that you both enjoyed it very much.*

▶ 3 Now listen to someone saying what they have done recently, and answer the following questions. You will hear the answers on the recording.

a What did Ana do with her family in Évora?
b What did she buy on Saturday?
c What did her friend eat in the new restaurant?
d At what time did Ana arrive home from work yesterday?
e What did she do before going to bed?

20

finalmente …

finally …

Congratulations; you have come to the end of the course. You have achieved a great deal so far. Learning a language on your own at home is no easy option, but having worked through this course, with the aid of the recording to improve your listening skills, you should now have enough confidence to try your Portuguese for real. In whichever Portuguese-speaking country you are, the inhabitants will welcome visitors who, like yourself, make an effort to speak the language. A whole new world can open up to you, as you see the faces of Portuguese people light up, and they'll ask, enthusiastically, **Fala português?** You will find that it's well worth the time and effort you have invested.

The Portuguese you have learnt in this course is the 'standard' language you'll hear among average eloquent speakers of the language. However, as you travel around Portugal (or if you visit other Portuguese-speaking countries), you will become aware of regional differences in accent, dialect and vocabulary. For example, the people of the Algarve tend to 'eat' their words a lot more than standard Portuguese speakers. In the Algarve both the beginning and the end of sentences can be muffled, or disappear almost completely, making it quite tricky to decipher. Often the word **obrigado** will sound like **briga**. The local expression for a bread roll in the Algarve is **papo-seco**, whereas the standard **pãozinho** is the norm in Lisbon. Don't let this alarm you; imagine a Portuguese person in the UK having to deal with bread roll, bap, barm cake, oven muffin, breakfast roll and so on! In rural areas, the speech is generally more drawn-out and melodic; in one part of the isolated northern regions, an old form of Latin is still found and is being revitalized. Be prepared for these differences and don't forget that they exist in every country. Don't be too rigid with what you have learnt so far. You have the best foundations to build on, but you need to be flexible enough to massage and modify as you go along.

As far as learning grammar is concerned, what you have encountered during this course is a basic grounding for simple, everyday conversations. In recent years grammar in language learning has been a taboo subject, but it is now recognized once more that with no grammatical structure learners cannot progress to form their own ideas and responses.

Verbs, of course, are the vital element in any language, and in Portuguese they are perhaps more complex than other Latin languages. In this course you have started talking about actions in the present tense, you have found an easy way of talking about the future, using the verb *to go*, and finally you have touched on the structure for two of the past tenses. To progress your learning and to prepare yourself for real conversations with Portuguese people, you now need to follow up with some further studying.

However, the most important thing about learning a language is to have constant contact with it in the spoken and written forms. Obviously the ideal would be to go and immerse yourself in the whole experience of living in Portugal. The next best thing is to discipline yourself to setting aside about ten to 15 minutes every day to practise. Recordings, videos, radio, satellite TV all help to improve the skill of listening. Reading is also essential so you could try to get hold of a Portuguese magazine or newspaper and glance through small articles for the gist only. Don't try to read a three-page article all at once as you will no doubt soon tire of it and become disillusioned. Bite-sized chunks are what is required. A little and often is the answer to learning. You could think of the process as a mental workout: would you try to run the marathon on your first day's run?

And so, where to from here? To improve on what you have already taken on board so well, you need a complete course, or, ideally, join a class where you can practise speaking with other people, and have the feedback from a teacher. Whatever you decide to do, remember to enjoy it, and have a great time trying it all out on your travels. **Boa Sorte!**

testing yourself

To help you monitor your progress with *Teach Yourself Beginner's Portuguese,* we have produced two self-assessment tests based on the units completed. **Test one** covers Units 1–10, and **Test two** covers 11–19. There is one exercise for every unit studied.

You will find the answers to the test questions in the **Key to the tests**, on pages 203–4. Where the questions require individual responses, we usually give you model answers to guide you.

We indicate the number of points allocated to each answer, so that you can keep your own score (out of a total of 70 points per test). Here are a few guidelines to help you grade your performance:

60–70 points	Congratulations! You have mastered the units very well indeed.
46–59 points	Very good. You have mastered most of the points covered in the units. Try to identify the areas which still need some work, and go over them again.
35–45 points	Well done, but it might be advisable to revise the areas where you are not so confident before moving on.
Below 35 points	Not a bad attempt, but it would be a good idea to go over the units again. When you have done that, take the test again and see how much you have improved.

Learning a new language always takes time, so don't panic if you have not been able to remember all the areas of each unit. Don't be discouraged – have a breather from it, and when you come back to it the next day it will begin to make more sense. And you will really start to see the difference when you put it into practice in the country.

Self-assessment test one: Units 1–10

The test covers the main vocabulary and phrases, skills and language points in these units. For how to read your score, refer back to page 186. You can check your answers on page 203. **Boa Sorte!** *Good Luck!*

1 Can you do the following? Say the answers out loud and also write them down. Two points for each correct answer.

   a Say 'good morning', and ask someone formally how they are.
   b Ask someone their name informally.
   c Give your own name.
   d Say how you are.
   e Say 'goodbye' and 'see you later'.

                                          Points: _____ / 10

2 Name these nationalities or languages:

   a brasileiro
   b espanhol
   c escocês
   d alemão
   e inglês.

                                          Points: _____ / 5

3 Verb endings: can you put the correct endings on to the stems of the verbs, according to who is doing the action?

-a	-am	-am	-o	-a	-amos

   a Eu mor_____.
   b Nós trabalh _____.
   c Ela pint _____.
   d Vocês fal _____.
   e O senhor and _____.
   f Eles estud _____.

                                          Points: _____ / 6

4 Members of the family – can you name them in English?

   a o pai   d a mulher
   b a filha   e os filhos
   c o irmão   f a mãe

                                          Points: _____ / 6

5 Describing places: can you find the missing letters to complete each adjective?

    a l _ m _ o   **d** hi _ _ ó _ i _ o
    b mov_ m _nt _ d _   **e** in_ e_ es _ an _ e.
    c c_l _ o

                                      Points: ____ / 5

6 Can you give five Portuguese words connected with houses (e.g rooms or what's in them)?

                                        Points: ____ / 5

7 Time: can you give these times?

    a midday   **d** 8.45
    b 2.10   **e** 4 p.m.
    c 6.30   **f** 7.55 a.m.

                                        Points: ____ / 6

8 Can you do the following? Two points each.

    a Say something you like to do in your free time.
    b Say how often you go to the supermarket.
    c Ask someone if they like listening to music.
    d Say what someone in your family likes to do.

                                        Points: ____ / 8

9 How many months of the year can you say / write accurately? One point for each correct answer.

                                      Points: ____ / 12

10 Can you say these in Portuguese?

    a by car   **e** for sale
    b I would like   **f** on the 9.30 plane
    c more than 20 euros **g** eat!
    d 200

                                        Points: ____ / 7

Self-assessment test two: Units 11–19

11 Can you do the following? Two points each.

    a Say 'is there a station here?'
    b Ask what time the train to Faro leaves.
    c Ask the Turismo for a list of hotels.
    d Ask someone formally if they know where the museum is.

e Say 'it's on the left'.
f Say 'take the first on the right'.

Points: ____ / 12

12 What do these signs mean?

a sanitários   d aberto
b fechado   e não fumar
c entrada   f saída de emergência.

Points: ____ / 6

13 Can you name in Portuguese:

three vegetables / three fruits / three fish / three meats / three general groceries / three items of clothing / three colours?

One point each.

Points: ____ / 21

14 What is on this menu?

> *pão e manteiga*   *salada e batatas fritas*
> *sopa de legumes*   *pudim flan*
> *sardinhas assadas*   *vinho tinto*

Points: ____ / 6

15 Unscramble the letters to find parts of the body

a BAEAÇC   d ABCO
b BORÇA   e MOÃ
c NRAEP

Points: ____ / 5

16 **Saber** vs **Conhecer** (*to know*): which verb would you use in these situations?

a She knows his name.
b I know the Mayor.
c Are you interested in getting to know Portugal?
d Do you know where something is?
e Jack doesn't know my sister.

Points: ____ / 5

17 Can you say the following?

a Do you have any rooms free?
b For two people.
c I'd like to reserve a room.
d I have a room reserved.
e The air-conditioning isn't working.

Points: ____ / 5

18 What are these weather conditions?

a vento   b sol   c frio   d chuva   e neve

Points: _____ / 5

19 Verbs in the simple past tense. Can you say the following?

a I spoke.   d We ate.
b You (*familiar*) made.   e They saw.
c He left.

Points: _____ / 5

taking it further

There follows a selection of information on further reading, websites, and other useful sources for learning Portuguese.

Reading

Vida Nova bilingual magzaine, subscriptions from 106 Victoria Road, London NW6 6QB

The Romance Languages, Martin Harris and Nigel Vincent (Routledge, 1997)

The Loom of Language, Frederick Bodmer (Allen & Unwin, 1946)

Dicionário Editora da Língua Portuguesa, a good monolingual dictionary (new edn. 1994)

Oxford–Duden Pictorial Dictionary, detailed visual vocabulary (1992)

Michaelis Dicionário Práctico, bilingual (English/Portuguese, both directions)

Collins Portuguese Dictionaries, various sizes.

The Babel Guide to the Fiction of Portugal, Brazil and Africa (Boulevard Books, 1995)

Learning

The BBC's *Talk Portuguese* series, first broadcast in 2003 and regularly repeated in BBC2's early-morning Learning Zone, has an associated website with slideshows, exercises and quizzes: www.bbc.co.uk/languages/other/portuguese/talk/index/shtml. Satellite TV, if you have access to it, will be able to reach Portuguese TV; there is an international channel called RTPi.

There are online courses, such as that offered by the University of Glasgow (UK), called *De tudo um pouco*.

Dicionário Universal da língua portuguesa is a CD-ROM version of a Portuguese dictionary (Texto Editora). Visit their website at: http://www.priberam.pt/DLPO.

Various CD-ROMs for learning Portuguese are now available from good bookstores.

Enrol on language courses at your local college / language school. Try to speak with Portuguese people when you are in Portugal – they will be grateful you have made an effort, and will encourage your attempts.

Places

Camões Institute, R. Rodrigues Sampaio 113, 115–279 Lisboa. Tel: 213-109-100 (see below for website)

Coordination of Portuguese Language Centres world-wide, Centro Coordenador dos Centros de Língua Portuguesa, Campo Grande 56, r/c, 1700-078 Lisboa. Tel: 217-956-113

Websites

There are many sites and materials in both English and Portuguese. Here are just a few ideas:

Camões Institute – language and cultural information:
    http:///www.instituto-camoes.pt
Comunidade de Países de Língua Portuguesa – Portuguese-speaking communities:
    http://www.cplp.org
Portugal and the Portuguese language:
    http://www.public.iastate.edu/~pedro/pt_connect.html
The Human Languages Page – materials, interesting links, institutions and information in the language of your choice:
    http://www.june29.com
King's College, London – Dept. of Portuguese and Brazilian studies, various links:
    http://www.kcl.ac.uk/depsta/humanities/pobrst/kclhp.htm
Língua Portuguesa – key this into search motor Altavista, and you should link to many more sites.
Grant & Cutler – stockists of Portuguese books in the UK:
    http://www.grantandcutler.com
For all sorts of information:
    http://www.portugal-info.net
Portuguese National Library:
    http://www.bn.pt/
Literature and language: www.portugalnet.pt

Publishers Lidel–Edições Técnicas Lda:
  http://www.lidel.pt
Publishers Porto Editora:
  http://www.portoeditora.pt
Portuguese bookshop:
  http://www.mediabooks.com

Many newspapers are available online; here is a selection:
  http://www.expresso.pt
  http://jn.sapo.pt/
  http://www.publico.pt
  http://www.euronoticias.pt

Radio and TV stations can also be found online; here are some:
  http://www.rdp.pt
  http://www.radiocomercial.iol.pt/
  http://www.rtp.pt

News site:
  http://www.diariodigital.pt/

Online magazine for women:
  http://www.mulherportuguesa.com/

Cinema:
  http://www.7arte.net

Unit 1

1 está / Estou / bem, obrigada / noite / até / Boa.
2 a Olá, bom dia. **b** Bom dia (*or* boa tarde *if after midday*). **c** Boa tarde, até amanhã. **d** Adeus (*or* Tchau), até logo / até já. **e** Olá, boa noite. **3 a** Boa tarde, estou bem obrigado/a. E o Nuno, como está? **b** Adeus (tchau), até amanhã.

Documento: Afternoon (**tarde**).

4 a Como se chama? **b** Como te chamas? **c** Como se chama (o senhor)? **5** Boa tarde / Olá / Bom dia / Adeus / Até logo / Até já. **6** Bom dia, como está? / Estou bem, obrigado, e a senhora? / Bem, obrigada. / Desculpe, como se chama? / Chamo-me Lúcia, e o senhor? / Eduardo./Muito prazer. / Igualmente

Self-evaluation: a Boa tarde, como está? **b** Boa noite, até à próxima. **c** Como te chamas? **d** Chamo-me . . . **e** Desculpe! **f** Muito prazer.

Unit 2

1 a Sou da (Inglaterra). **b** Sou (inglês / inglesa). **c** De onde é Senhor Silva? **d** A Ana é brasileira. **e** De onde são (Sr e Senhora Brito)? **f** O Paulo é da Itália. **g** O Senhor e a Senhora McDonald são escoceses.
2 a portuguesa, **b** Alemanha, **c** americanas, **d** ingleses, **e** Itália, **f** escocês. **3 b** Os senhores Schmidt são alemães. Eles são da Alemanha. **c** A Ellen e a Mary são dos Estados Unidos. Elas são americanas. **d** A Sandra, o John e a Brenda são da Inglaterra. Eles são ingleses. **e** O Marco

Giovanni é italiano. Ele é da Itália. **f** O Mac é da Escócia. Ele é escocês. **4 a** Fala italiano? **b** Não sou americano/a. **c** Falo português e inglês. **d** Fala português? **e** Não sou alemão/ã, mas falo alemão. **5 a** Falso, **b** Verdadeiro, **c** Verdadeiro, **d** Verdadeiro, **e** Falso. **6 a** Sim, falo um pouco. **b** Não, não sou alemão/ã, sou (inglês/a). **c** Sim, falo inglês e (também) italiano. **d** Obrigado/a, adeus.

Documento 1: a English, **b** German, Italian.
Documento 2: English, Portuguese, German.

Self-evaluation: a De onde é, Paulo? **b** Sou da (Inglaterra). **c** (o senhor Mendes) é brasileiro? **d** De onde são? **e** Somos (ingleses / inglesas). **f** A Júlia é portuguesa. **g** O João é dos Estados Unidos? **h** Fala inglês? **i** Não, não falo alemão. **j** Sim, sou inglês / inglesa.

Unit 3

1 a Onde mora (vive) Senhora Gomes? **b** Moro (vivo) na Inglaterra. **c** A Maria mora (vive) na praça. **d** Onde moram os senhores? **e** (O Renato) vive na Alemanha? **2 a** A Lúcia mora na avenida. **b** Nós moramos na rua. **c** Mora no beco. **d** Eles moram na praça. **3 a** iii, **b** iv, **c** i, **d** ii, **e** v.

Documento: Pastelaria Antiqua.

4 a Onde trabalha senhor Gomes? **b** Sou estudante. **c** O que faz, José? **d** Trabalho num/a . . . **e** Não trabalho. **5 a** cinco, **b** doze, **c** treze, **d** dezoito, **e** dois, **f** dezanove. **6 a** Universidade, **b** banco, **c** empresa, **d** aeroporto, **e** escritório, **f** escola.

Self-evaluation: b Onde moram os senhores? **c** Moro em (Lancaster). **d** Moro numa rua / praça / avenida. **e** Moro numa casa moderna. **f** Onde trabalha? **g** O que faz? **h** Sou (professora) **i** Trabalho numa (escola).

Unit 4

1 a o meu irmão. **b** a nossa mãe. **c** a sua filha. **d** os nossos filhos. **e** o meu pai. **2 a** A Ana é a filha mais nova. **b** O Miguel é o nosso irmão mais alto. **c** Eles são os meus filhos mais velhos. **d** o António é mais baixo. **e** a Maria e a Paula são mais altas. **3 a** Chama-se Rosa. **b** Trabalha numa escola secundária. **c** É o Roberto.

d É muito calma. **e** Trabalha num hospital. **f** Não, é alto.
4 **a** Tem uma filha? **b** Temos dois filhos. **c** Ela tem um
irmão? **d** Tenho uma irmã. **e** Têm filhos? **5**
Preguiçoso, elegante, desportivo, barulhento, sério, calmo,
nervoso, honesto.

Documento: Age up to 25, not a student, artistic.

6 Quantos anos tem a sua filha? Ela tem onze anos.

Self-evaluation: **a** Este é o meu marido / esta é a minha
mulher. **b** Aquele é o meu irmão / aquela é a minha irmã.
c Esté é o nosso filho / esta é a nossa filha **d** Aquela é a
minha irmã mais nova. **e** O meu marido é (sério) /a minha
mulher é (honesta) / o meu professor é (calmo). **f** Sou
(alegre). **g** Quantos anos tem? **h** Tenho (x) anos.

Unit 5

1 **a** Os senhores Brito gostam de frango? **b** Não gostas do
caldo verde? **c** Não, não gosto. **d** Gostamos muito
(imenso) de sardinhas. **e** a Paula gosta um pouco de arroz de
marisco. **f** Gostam imenso da comida portuguesa. **2** **a** a,
b o, **c** amos, **d** as, **e** am. **3** **a** iii, **b** i, **c** v, **d** ii,
e iv.

Documento 1: Seafood rice (Arroz de Marisco).

4 **a** Sim. Gosta. **b** Porque é um país muito limpo.
c Porque tem um clima agradável. **d** Não, não gostam
muito. **e** A mulher do Nuno prefere a Dinamarca.
f Porque preferem o barulho.

Documento 2: Something different.

5 **a** Prefiro a Inglaterra porque é histórica. **b** O senhor
Antunes prefere a Suíça ou a Dinamarca? **c** A Sônia prefere
a Itália porque é interessante. **d** Qual preferem (os
senhores), os Estados Unidos, ou o Japão? **e** Preferimos a
Holanda porque é bonita. **6** Velho / movimentado /
desagradável / caro / sujo / calmo / limpo.

Self-evaluation:
a Gosta de frango? **b** Gosto um pouco de sardinhas.
c O Miguel gosta imenso da comida portuguesa. **d** O
Senhor não gosta do caldo verde? **e** Prefiro Portugal porque
é interessante. **f** Qual preferem – a Itália ou o Japão?
g Preferimos a comida dinamarquesa.

Unit 6

1 a Ana Maria's, b Roberto's. 2 típica / três / pequenos / grande / terraço / há / casa de banho / baixo / cozinha / de / sala de jantar. 3 [*Typical answer*]: A minha casa é uma casa moderna. Fica num bairro moderno. Na casa há dois quartos em cima, e uma cozinha e uma sala de estar em baixo. Gosto da minha casa. 4 a Em frente da lareira. b Um vaso de flores. c Debaixo da mesa. d Sim, há. e Um quadro bonito e um armário. f Não; há um chuveiro. 5 a Falso, b Falso, c Falso, d Verdadeiro, e Falso, f Verdadeiro. 6 a O gato está em cima do frigorífico. b Há um armário ao lado da estante. c Há um sofá detrás da mesa? d O chuveiro não está na cozinha. e O fogão está ao lado da máquina de lavar. f O gato está em frente da poltrona? 7 1T 2T 3T 4F 5F.

Documento· a Three, b Yes.

Self-evaluation: a (e.g.) Tenho um apartamento moderno. b (e.g.) A minha casa tem . . . uma cozinha . . . . c Como é a sua casa? d Tenho uma cozinha / casa de banho grande / pequena. e Há dois / três / quatro / cinco quartos. f Não há uma sala de estar / sala de jantar. g (e.g.) O sofá está ao lado da mesa. h (e.g.) O frigorífico está na cozinha. i O que há no quarto?

Unit 7

1 a levanta-se, b 9 horas, c janta / sete menos um quarto, d aula de japonês, e à uma. 2 a iii, b vi c iv, d i, e v, f ii. 3 a iii, b i, c iv, d ii, e v. 4 [*Sample answers*] a Levanto-me às 7 horas. b Almoço ao meio-dia. c Chego em casa às 5 e meia. d Deito-me às 10 e um quarto.

Documento: Wednesday a.m. (4ª feira de manhã)

5 a Levanto-me cedo. b Ele não se deita tarde. c A que horas se vestem? d Não nos vestimos rapidamente. e Como se chamam? f A que horas te levantas? 6 a compreende, b parte, c comemos, d vivem, e abres, f bebe.

Self-evaluation: b A que horas se levanta? d Não nos deitamos até às 10 e meia. e A que horas almoça nos / aos domingos (Paulo)? f Não como muito nas / às terças. g A que horas vai à igreja Jorge? h Que horas são?

Unit 8

1 **a** Maria, o que gosta de fazer no tempo livre? **b** Gosto de costurar. **c** Os Senhores gostam de viajar? **d** Gostam de praticar desportos? **e** (e.g.) Não gosto de dançar.
f Gostas de nadar no tempo livre? **2** **a** Sim, claro.
b Não, não somos portugueses, somos ingleses. Somos de . . . (Manchester). **c** Sim, falo um pouco de português. **d** Gosto de ir ao teatro. **e** O meu marido / a minha mulher gosta de trabalhar no jardim, e os meus filhos gostam de praticar desportos. **f** Sim, claro!

Documento 1: Yes.

3 livros / leio / dias / vejo / ouve / joga / nunca / lê / gosta / vão / todas / vez / quando / fazem. **4** **a** iii, **b** vi, **c** iv, **d** i, **e** v, **f** ii. **5** **a** cada dia, **b** uma vez por mês **c** de vez em quando **d** muitas vezes, **e** nunca, **f** às vezes, **g** todos os dias.

Documento 2: Every day.

6 1 c 2 a 3 b 4 a.

Self-evaluation: **a** O que gosta de fazer no tempo livre?
b (e.g.) Gosto de dançar. **c** Claro que pode. **d** O meu marido / a minha mulher gosta de . . . **e** Vejo a televisão (todos os dias . . .) **f** Ouvem muitas vezes a música?
g Vou à cidade para fazer compras.

Unit 9

Reading: **1** Na ilha do Paraíso. **2** Andar. **3** No mar, três piscinas. **4** Ténis, piscinas, campo de golfe e desportos aquáticos. **5** A oportunidade de relaxar num ambiente natural e especial.

1 **a** Vou muitas vezes para a Itália na primavera. **b** Gosto da cultura italiana. **c** O nosso filho sempre vem connosco, mas a nossa filha prefere viajar com o namorado. **d** Em geral ficamos em casa, mas eu e a minha família queremos conhecer a França no outono. **2** **a** sei, **b** conhece, **c** sabem, **d** conhecem, **e** sei, **f** sabemos. **3** [*possible answers*] **a** Eu vou tirar férias em Abril. **b** Tu vais viajar pela Escócia no ano que vem. **c** Você vai visitar o meu amigo amanhã. **d** Nós vamos trabalhar no jardim no sábado.
e Os Senhores vão nadar no mar em Julho. **f** Eles vão jogar golfe na sexta-feira. **5** **a** Gostaria de visitar a Alemanha.

b O Paulo não gostaria de trabalhar na segunda-feira.
c Gostariam de beber connosco? **d** O meu marido / a minha mulher gostaria de provar a comida brasileira. **e** Gostaríamos de viajar pelos Estados Unidos. **5** All months – check list on page 93

Documento: end June–September

6 **a** Verdadeiro, **b** Falso, **c** Falso, **d** Verdadeiro, **e** Verdadeiro.

Self-evaluation: **a** Onde vão passar as férias este ano? **b** Quero conhecer a Grécia. **c** A minha família sempre passa as férias em Portugal. **d** Sabe nadar? **e** (e.g.) No ano que vem vou passar as férias na Itália. **f** Quer vir também?

Unit 10

1 geral / de / volto / dias / barato / rápido / fins / fora / vou / gosto / bicicleta / férias / barco / avião. **2** 862 / 1,241 / 349 / 2,766 / 299 / 758 / 5,512 / 10, 150 / 683 / 3,371.

Documento: 23747 / 29624.

Reading: **1** Bicicleta. **2** Bonita. **3** Passear no campo, chegar mais rápido ao trabalho e melhorar a saúde. **4** 20 euros. **5** Barata.

3 **a** Vou ao trabalho no carro do meu amigo (da minha amiga). **b** O Paulo vai ao hospital de autocarro. **c** A Ana viaja no comboio das 2 e meia. **d** O senhor e a senhora da Costa vão de férias de barco. **e** Vamos ao cinema no autocarro das 7.15. **f** Viajas de avião? **4** **a** compre, **b** comam, **c** partam **d** viaje, **e** falem, **f** beba. **5** car 1, coach 2, bicycle 3, horse 4, bus 5, on foot 6.

Self-evaluation: **a** Como se chama? **b** Muito prazer. **c** Sou inglesa, sou de Morecambe. [*Sample answer only*] **d** O meu marido/a minha mulher fala português. **e** Onde moram? **f** Trabalho numa universidade; sou professora. **g** Tenho 30 anos. **h** O meu pai é alto, e honesto. **i** Gostas de café? **j** Prefiro a França. **k** A minha casa é um apartamento antigo. **l** O sofá/a mesa/o armário está ao lado de . . . **m** Que horas são? **n** Levanto-me às 7 horas, vou ao trabalho, volto para casa às 5.30, janto às 7, e deito-me às 11. **o** Gostam de viajar? **p** No tempo livre gosto de ler. **q** Onde passa as férias? **r** Eu e a minha família gostaríamos de visitar a Espanha. **s** Como vai ao trabalho? **t** !!!!! And take your time.

Unit 11

1 a Há autocarros para Lisboa? b A paragem de autocarros é ali à esquerda. c O ponto de táxis é ali à direita. d A que horas parte o comboio para Faro? e Às seis e 15 da tarde. f A que horas chega o barco? g Há um aeroporto aqui? h O terminal é ali, em frente. i Para o porto, sc faz favor. 2 a Boa tarde, queria dois bilhetes para Loulé, se faz favor. b De ida e volta, por favor. c Primeira. Qual é a linha para Loulé? d A que horas parte o comboio? e E a que horas chega? f Obrigado/a.

Documento: a single, b 2nd.

3 a Sim, b Castelo / catedral. c peixe / mariscos / sardinhas / doces de amêndoa e figo. d Quinta de Lago, e Não. f de pescadores. 4 a Vire à esquerda, siga em frente, e o banco fica à esquerda na esquina. b Vire aqui à esquerda, e depois à esquerda. Tome a terceira rua à esquerda, e siga em frente. O mercado fica à direita. c Vá em frente e vire à direita. Tome a primeira à direita e siga até à estação que fica em frente. d Vire à esquerda e depois à direita. Siga em frente, pela praça Dom João até à Rua 5 de Outubro. Depois, vire à esquerda e vá em frente. O Turismo é ali à direita. 5 a mercado, b estação, c Turismo

6 O mercado vìra / à direita / toma / primeria / à esquerda / segue em frente / à esqina / o mercado / mesmo ali

Unit 12

1 i b; ii d; iii a; iv c; v e.

Notices: a for children, b no smoking, c no parking, d open from 10–12, e danger, f emergency exit, g no entry, h closed.

Documento: a Park between 1 and 3 p.m. b It's an emergency exit.
2 1 esterlinas, 2 passaporte, 3 morada, 4 selos, 5 euros, 6 levantar, 7 cartas, 8 cabine.

Unit 13

Wordsearch: melancia / banana / repolho / espadarte / laranja / carapau / pêra / lulas / javali / pimentão
1 a cenouras, b porco, c presunto, d bolachas, e sopa, f água, g pasta de dentes, h ovos.

Documento: Yes.

2 a Vários lugares – feira, centro comercial, casa de moda. **b** Sim. **c** Não. **d** Uma blusa. **e** Azul. **f** Preto. **g** De salto alto. **h** Sim, gosta. **3 a** Bom dia. Queria um litro de água e um pão de forma. **b** Não faz mal. Levo um. Tem presunto? **c** Então, pode cortar-me seis fatias, se faz favor. **d** Quero também uma lata de ervilhas e uma barra de sabão. **e** É tudo, obrigado/a. Quanto é?

Unit 14

1 a Paulo: uma bica, uma sandes de fiambre, um pastel de nata. **b** Nuno: um galão, sandes de queijo, pastel de bacalhau, pastel de nata. **c** Ana: bica, sandes de fiambre, 2 pastéis de bacalhau. **d** Maria: pingado, sandes de fiambre, 2 pastéis de nata. **e** Miguel: bica, pastel de bacalhau, pastel de nata. **2 a** frango, **b** exótica, **c** mexicale, **d** quatro estações, **e** neptuno **3 a** open every day, **b** 11.30–24.00 (Friday / Saturday / National Holidays open till 2 a.m.) **c** on Mondays. **d** O que vais escolher? **e** Acho que quero uma pizza de frango. **f** Tens muita fome! **g** Não bebes nada? **h** Vou pedir uma 7-Up. **i** Queres um refrigerante? **j** Quero uma dose de batatas fritas. **4 a** Boa noite, tem sopa? **b** Queria um caldo verde. **c** Queria meia dose do bacalhau. Vem com salada? **d** Está bem. **e** Pode ser o pudim flan. **f** Pode ser meia gerrafa de vinho branco e depois, uma bica. **5** (A) 10, 13 (B) 1, 16 (C) 2, 15, 18 (D) 7, 9, 12, 19 (E) 4, 8, 11, 17, 20 (F) 3, 5, 6, 14

Documento: Wine / water.

Person	Name of item	Quantity	Price
1	onions	1 kilo	€1.25
2	ham	6 slices	50 cêntimos
3	honey	2 jars	90 cêntimos
4	eggs	10	90 cêntimos
5	sardines	½ kilo	€1.79

Unit 15

1 a tenho uma dor de garganta. **b** A minha filha cortou o dedo. **c** Doem-me os ouvidos. **d** O meu marido tem insolação. **e** Creio que o meu filho vai vomitar. **f** Bati o dedo do pé. **g** A minha amiga magoou a perna.

2 [*Example of completed form*]

George Robert Smith
68
10/3/40
Newcastle, Inglaterra.
26 Church Row, Leicester, UK
01634-921550.
(passport) LL01652B3.
NH5288316.
Mrs J. Green, 43 Market Street
Oxford, UK

Documento: Throat.

Reading: 1 7950608. 2 Non-emergency calls.
3 National Help No. (=999). 4 424124. 5 If there's a fire
(bombeiros=firemen).
Ex3 1T 2T 3F 4F 5T.

Unit 16

1 a conhece, b sabemos, c conhecer, d conhecem,
e sabe.

2 a Este é o caminho certo para Lisboa? b Vai demorar
muito? c O meu carro está avariado. d Preciso dum
reboque. e Quero 8 litros de gasolina sem chumbo.
f Aceita cartões de crédito? g Pode encher o depósito.
3 a Sim. b uma caixa de Pronto – Socorros. c Não.
d Observar um limite de velocidade de 90 q.p.h / expor um
autocolante ao vidro do carro. e 90 q.p.h. 4 pneu /
gasolina / óleo / depósito / estrada / reboque /
travões / avariado.

Unit 17

1 a Tem quartos vagos? b Somos três. c Queria reservar
um quarto individual. d É a pensão Sol? e Qual é o preço
com pequeno almoço?

Documento: a 2 people b free.
2 i b; ii d; iii a; iv c; v e.

Leitura: 1 areas of rare beauty. 2 32. 3 personal.
4 regional, the best of. 5 meaning of the art and pleasure of
travel.
3 a Tem quartos vagos para hoje? b Somos três.
c Vamos ficar duas noites. d Queríamos um quarto de casal
e um quarto individual. e Sim, se faz favor; qual é o preço?

Unit 18

1 a Sim. **b** Não. **c** do lago. **d** a chuva pinga em cima das tendas. **e** o fundo do parque. **f** 8 dias. **g** tudo – mercearias, jornais, garrafas de gás, coberturas impermeáveis. **h** 7.30 da manhã.

Documento: i autocarro. **ii** tenda pequena. **iii** caravana. **iv** carro-cama. **v** tenda grande. **vi** automóvel.
2 a F, **b** V, **c** F, **d** V, **e** F, **f** V.
Reading: 1F; 2V; 3V; 4F; 5V; 6F

3 a iii, **b** vi, **c** iv, **d** i, **e** v, **f** ii. **4 a** Vai fazer calor.
b Vai fazer sol. **c** Faz frio. **d** Vai chover. **e** Há vento.
f Está a nevar (há neve).
5 1b 2a 3b 4b.

Unit 19

1a [*Possible answers*]: **i** O Paulo foi ao parque. **ii** Tu viste o filme. **iii** Eu e a Maria visitámos a cidade. **iv** Vocês fizeram muitas coisas interessantes. **v** Eu trabalhei ontem.
1b i Vamos ao parque hoje? **ii** Quero jogar futebol.
iii O que fizeste ontem? **iv** Fui à praia. **v** Gostou do parque, John?

Reading: Mother: Activity 2; Father: 6; Brother: 4; Sisters: 5; Grandparents: 7.

2 a A semana passada eu e a minha irmã visitámos Lisboa.
b Fomos a um palácio e vimos muitas coisas interessantes.
c Não, comemos num café na praça. **d** Sim, gostámos muito.

3 a Strolled in the park with her family and walked through the town centre, **b** a blouse and some sandals, **c** chicken, **d** 7.30 p.m., **e** watched a little television

Key to the tests

1 a Bom dia, como está? **b** Como te chamas? **c** Chamo-me (Sue) **d** (Estou bem.) **e** Adeus, até logo.

2 a Brazilian, **b** Spanish, **c** Scottish, **d** German, **e** English.

3 a moro, **b** trabalhamos, **c** pinta, **d** falam, **e** anda, **f** estudam.

4 a father, **b** daughter, **c** brother, **d** wife, **e** sons / children, **f** mother.

5 a limpo, b movimentado, c calmo, d histórico,
   e interessante.

6 *For example:* cozinha / sala de estar / sala de jantar / casa
   de banho / quarto / terraço etc. For more ideas see Unit 6.

7 a meio-dia, b duas e dez, c seis e meia, d nove menos um
   quarto *or* menos quinze, e quatro horas, (da tarde) f oito
   menos cinco (da manhã).

8 a (Gosto de ir nadar.) b Vou ao supermercado (todos os
   sábados). c Gosta de escutar música? d (O meu marido
   gosta de andar de bicicleta.)

9 See Unit 9 for all months.

10 a de carro, b queria, c mais de vinte euros, d duzentos, e
   vende-se, f no avião das nove e meia, g coma! *or* come! *or*
   comam!

11 a Há uma estação de comboios *or* de caminho de ferro
   aqui? b A que horas sai o comboio para Faro? c Tem uma
   lista de hotéis? d Sabe onde fica o museu? e Fica / É à
   esquerda f Tome a primeira à direita.

12 a toilets, b closed, c entrance, d open, e no smoking, f
   emergency exit.

13 See Unit 13 for examples.

14 bread and butter / vegetable soup / grilled (roast) sardines /
   salad and chips / crème caramel / red wine.

15 a cabeça, b braço, c perna, d boca, e mão.

16 a saber, b conhecer, c conhecer, d saber, e conhecer.

17 a Tem quartos vagos? b Para duas pessoas. c Queria
   reservar um quarto. d Tenho um quarto reservado. e O ar-
   condicionado não está a funcionar / não funciona.

18 a wind, b sun, c cold, d rain, e snow.

19 a falei, b fizeste, c partiu, d comemos, e viram.

Portuguese–English vocabulary

à direita *on the right*
à esquerda *on the left*
a pé *on foot*
aborrecido/a *boring*
aceita *accept*
advogado/a *lawyer*
aeroporto (o) *airport*
agora *now*
agradável *agreeable*
ajuda (a) *help*
albergue (o) *hostel, inn*
alguém *someone*
ambiente (o) *atmosphere*
amigos (os) *friends*
andar (o) *floor*
anos (os) *years*
antigo/a *old*
ao fundo *at the back*
ao lado de *next to*
aos sábados *on Saturdays*
apanhar sol *to sunbathe*
apanhar *to catch*
apartamento (o) *apartment*
aquecimento (o) *heating*
aquele/aquela *that*
aqui *here*
ar (o) *air*
areia (a) *sand*
armário (o) *wardrobe, cupboard*
arranjar *to arrange*
arroz de marisco (o) *seafood rice*

artístico/a *artistic*
árvores (as) *trees*
às vezes *sometimes*
ascensor (o) *lift*
aspirina (a) *aspirin*
assim *so, thus*
assinar *to sign*
assoalhadas (as) *rooms*
até *until, up to*
até breve *see you soon*
atracções (as) *attractions*
atrelado (o) *trailer*
autocarro (o) *bus*
avaria (a) *break-down*
avariado/a *broken down*
avenida (a) *avenue*
avião (o) *aeroplane*
azeite (o) *olive oil*

bacalhau (o) *salted cod*
banco (o) *bank*
banqueiro/a *bank clerk*
barato/a *cheap*
barco (o) *boat*
barulhento/a *noisy*
barulho (o) *noise*
bastante *quite*
bem *well*
biblioteca (a) *library*
bica (a) *espresso coffee*
bicicleta (a) *bicycle*

bilhete (o) *ticket*
blusa (a) *blouse*
boleia (a) *lift*
bonito/a *pretty*
botas (as) *boots*
buraco (o) *hole*

cá *here*
cabedal (o) *leather*
cabine (a) *phone booth*
cada ... *every ...*
caixa (a) *cash desk, till*
calças (as) *trousers*
caldo verde (o) *kale soup*
calmo/a *calm*
cama (a) *bed*
caminho (o) *way, road*
camioneta (a) *coach*
camisa (a) *shirt*
campo de golfe (o) *golf course*
campo (o) *countryside*
caravana (a) *caravan*
carne (a) *meat*
caro/a *expensive*
carro (o) *car*
carro-cama (o) *camper-van*
carta (a) *letter*
carteira (a) *wallet, purse*
casa de banho (a) *bathroom*
casa de modas (a) *fashion house*
casa (a) *house*
casal (o) *couple, double*
cavalo (o) *horse*
cedo *early*
cenouras (as) *carrots*
centro (o) *centre*
certo/a *correct*
céu (o) *sky*
chamada (a) *phone call*
chamo-me *my name is*
charmoso/a *charming*
chefe *boss*
chega *arrives*
cheio de *full of*

chuva (a) *rain*
chuveiro (o) *shower*
cidade (a) *town, city*
claro *of course*
clima (o) *climate*
coisa (a) *thing*
colecção (a) *collection*
com *with*
comboio (o) *train*
come *he/she eats*
comemos *we eat*
comida (a) *food*
como é? *what is it like?*
como está? *how are you?*
completamente *completely*
comprar *to buy*
compras (as) *shopping*
comprimido (o) *pill*
comunicar *to report*
conduzir *to drive*
conhecer *to get to know*
conjunto (o) *suit*
connosco *with us*
contra *against*
cor (a) *colour*
correio (o) *post office*
cozinha (a) *cuisine / kitchen*
creio *I believe, think*
criança (a) *child*
cuidado *careful*
cultura (a) *culture*
cultural *cultural*
custa *it costs*

de nada *don't mention it*
de onde é? *where are you from?*
de onde são? *where are you from? (pl.)*
de vez em quando *sometimes*
debaixo de *underneath*
deixar *to leave*
delicioso/a *delicious*
dentista (o) *dentist*
depois *then, after*

desagradável *unpleasant*
desculpa *excuse me*
desempregado/a *unemployed*
desmaiar *to faint*
desportivo/a *sporty*
desportos (os) *sports*
detrás de *behind*
difícil *difficult*
Dinamarca (a) *Denmark*
dinheiro (o) *money*
diz *says*
dona de casa (a) *housewife*
dormir *to sleep*
dose (a) *portion*
durante *during*
dúzia (a) *dozen*

e *and*
é *is*
elegante *elegant*
elevador (o) *lift*
em *in, on*
em baixo *downstairs, below*
em cima de *on top of*
em cima *upstairs, above*
em família *as a family*
em frente de *in front of*
em geral *generally*
empresa (a) *business, company*
encher *to fill*
enfermeiro/a *nurse*
então *well then*
entre *in between*
escola (a) *school*
escritor/a *writer*
escritório (o) *office*
Espanha (a) *Spain*
espanhóis *Spanish* (pl.)
esquina (a) *corner*
está boa? *are you well?*
estação (a) *station*
estacionado/a *parked*
estante (a) *bookcase*
estás bom? *are you well?*

este/esta *this*
estilo (o) *style*
estou bem *I'm well*
estou óptimo/a *I'm fine*
estrada (a) *highway*
estudante *student*
eu *I*
exactamente *exactly*
experimentar *to try on*

fácil *easy*
fala? *do you speak?*
falo *I speak*
família (a) *family*
faz favor de... *please...*
feijoada (a) *bean stew*
férias (as) *holidays*
fiambre (o) *ham*
fica *is situated*
ficar *to stay, be (situated)*
ficha (a) *form*
filha (a) *daughter*
filho (o) *son*
flores (as) *flowers*
fogão (o) *cooker*
fome (a) *hunger*
fora *outside*
forno (o) *oven*
França (a) *France*
frango (o) *chicken*
freguês/esa *customer*
fresco/a *cooled*
frigorífico (o) *fridge*
funcionar *to work*
furo (o) *puncture*

galão (o) *milky coffee*
garrafa (a) *bottle*
gasóleo (o) *diesel*
gasolina (a) *petrol*
gato (o) *cat*
gente (a) *people*
geralmente *generally*
gosta/am? *do you like?*

gostam *they like*
gostamos *we like*
gostaria de *I would like to*
gosto *I like*
grande *big*
gravata (a) *tie*
Grécia (a) *Greece*

há *there is, are*
há meia hora *½ hour ago*
havia *there was, were*
histórico/a *historical*
hoje *today*
Holanda (a) *Holland*
honesto/a *honest*
hotel (o) *hotel*

ida e volta (a) *return (ticket)*
ida (a) *single (ticket)*
idade (a) *age*
ideal *ideal*
igreja (a) *church*
igualmente *likewise*
ilha (a) *island*
imenso *a lot*
incluindo *including*
informações (as) *information*
inglês/esa *English*
inteiro/a *whole*
interessante *interesting*
inverno (o) *winter*
ir *to go*
irmã (a) *sister*
irmão (o) *brother*
isolado/a *isolated*

Japão (o) *Japan*
jaqueta (a) *jacket*
jogar *to play*
jornais (os) *newspapers*
jovem *young*
lá fora *out there*
lá, ali *there*
lago (o) *lake*

lama (a) *mud*
lamento *I'm sorry*
laranjas (as) *oranges*
lareira (a) *fireplace*
leio *I read*
leite (o) *milk*
ler *to read*
levo *I'll take*
libras (as) *pounds*
limpar *to clean*
limpo/a *clean*
linha (a) *platform*
lista (a) *list, menu*
litro (o) *litre*
livros (os) *books*
loja (a) *shop*
Londres *London*
longe *a long way*
lugar (o) *place*

maçada (a) *pain, drag*
maduro/a *ripe*
mãe (a) *mother*
maior *bigger*
mais de *more than*
mais ou menos *more or less*
mais tarde *later*
manteiga (a) *butter*
mapa (o) *map*
máquina de lavar (a) *washing machine*
máquina fotográfica (a) *camera*
mar (o) *sea*
maravilhoso/a *wonderful*
marido (o) *husband*
mariscos (os) *seafood*
mas *but*
médico/a *doctor*
meio quilo *half a kilo*
melhorar *to improve*
mercearias (as) *groceries*
mesa (a) *table*
mesmo ali *right there*
moderno/a *modern*

molhado/a *wet*
mora *he/she/it/you live(s)*
morada (a) *address*
moram *they, you live*
moro *I live*
mosquitos (os) *mosquitoes*
movimentado/a *busy*
muitas vezes *often*
muito *very*
muito bem *very well*
muito prazer *pleased to meet you*
mulher (a) *wife*
museu (o) *museum*
música (a) *music*

na *in / on the*
nadar *to swim*
namorado/a *boy/girlfriend*
não *no*
não funciona *it doesn't work*
nervoso/a *nervous*
neve (a) *snow*
nome (o) *name*
nos arredores *on the outskirts*
número (o) *number*
nunca *never*

o que faz? *what do you do?*
objectos (os) *objects*
obrigado/a *thank you*
oferece *offers*
óleo (o) *oil*
ontem *yesterday*
oportunidade (a) *opportunity*
ora bem! *well now!*
organizar *to organize*
orgulhoso/a *proud*
ou ... ou ... *either ... or ...*
ouço *I listen to*
outono (o) *autumn*
outros (os) *the others*
ouvir *to listen to*
ovos (os) *eggs*

pacote (o) *packet*
padrão (o) *style*
pai (o) *father*
país (o) *country*
pais (os) *parents*
pão (o) *bread*
par (o) *pair*
para *in order to*
para nós *for us*
para o ano *next year*
paragem (a) *bus stop*
parede (a) *wall*
parque (o) de campismo *camping
   park*
parque (o) *park*
parte *departs*
partido/a *broken*
passamos *we spend*
passaporte (o) *passport*
passar *to pass*
passear *to stroll*
pastelaria (a) *cake shop*
pedir *to ask for*
pelo menos *at least*
pensão (a) *guest house*
pequeno/a *small*
pêras (as) *pears*
perigoso/a *dangerous*
perto *near*
pessoalmente *personally*
picado/a *stung*
pingar *to drip*
pintar *to paint*
piquenique (o) *picnic*
piscina (a) *swimming pool*
planta (a) *town plan*
podem *you (pl.) can*
podemos *we can*
pode-se *you (one) can*
pois *well*
poltrona (a) *armchair*
pôr *to put*
por noite *per night*
por favor *please*

porque *because*
porta (a) *door*
portanto *therefore*
porto (o) *port*
português/esa *Portuguese*
posso? *may I?*
postal (o) *postcard*
poucas vezes *few times, seldom*
pouquinho (um) *a little bit*
praça (a) *square*
praia (a) *beach*
preciso de *I need*
preço (o) *price*
prédio (o) *building*
preencher *to fill in*
prefere *he she, you prefer(s)*
preferem *they, you prefer*
preferimos *we prefer*
prefiro *I prefer*
preguiçoso/a *lazy*
presunto (o) *smoked ham*
primavera (a) *spring*
primeiro/a *first*
problema (o) *problem*
professor/ora *teacher*
protecção (a) *protection*
provar *to try, taste*
provavelmente *probably*
próximo *nearby*

quadra de ténis *tennis court*
quadro (o) *picture*
qual? *which?*
qualidade (a) *quality*
qualquer coisa *something*
quanto é? *how much is it?*
quantos/as *how many?*
quarto (o) *¼ litre bottle*
quarto (o) *bedroom*
que *that, which*
que mais? *what else?*
que tal? *how about?*
queijo (o) *cheese*
quem? *who?*

quer *he/she/it/you want(s)*
quilo (o) *kilo*
quinze dias *fortnight*
quotidiano/a *everyday*

rápido/a *fast*
reboque (o) *lift, tow*
recepção (a) *reception*
recomendo *I recommend*
refeições (as) *meals*
reformado/a *retired*
refrigerante (o) *soft drink*
região (a) *region*
relaxante *relaxing*
remédio (o) *medicine*
repolho (o) *cabbage*
reservado/a *reserved*
reservar *to reserve*
resto (o) do dia *the rest of the day*
reunião (a) *meeting*
revistas (as) *magazines*
rotunda (a) *roundabout*
roubo (o) *theft*
roupas (as) *clothes*
rua (a) *road*

saia (a) *skirt*
saída (a) *exit*
sal (o) *salt*
sala de estar (a) *living room*
sala de jantar (a) *dining room*
sala (a) *living room*
salto alto (, de) *high heeled*
sandálias (as) *sandals*
sandes (a) *sandwich*
sapatos (os) *shoes*
sardinhas (as) *sardines*
saudável *healthy*
saúde (a) *health*
se *if*
se calhar *probably*
selo (o) *stamp*
sem *without*
sempre *always*

senhores (os) *you*
sentar-se *to sit down*
sentir-se *to feel*
sério/a *serious*
sim *yes*
simpático/a *nice*
sinais (os) *road signs*
sintoma (o) *symptom*
sobremesa (a) *dessert*
sofá (o) *sofa*
solitário/a *lonely*
sombra (a) *shade*
somos *we are*
sossego (o) *quiet*
sou *I am*
sou de *I am from*
sozinho/a *alone*
Suíça (a) *Switzerland*
sujo/a *dirty*
sumo (o) *fruit juice*

talvez haja *perhaps there may be*
tamanho (o) *size*
também *also*
tarde (a) *afternoon*
táxi (o) *taxi*
telenovelas (as) *soap-operas*
televisão (a) *television*
têm *they have*
tem ...? *do you have ...?*
temos *we have*
tempo de lazer (o) *leisure time*
tempo livre (o) *free time*
tenda (a) *tent*
tenho *I have*
terceiro/a *third*
terminal (o) *bus terminus*
terra (a) *land, hometown*
terraço (o) *balcony*
tipicamente *typically*

típico/a *typical*
tirar férias *to take a holiday*
todas as noites *every night*

todos os dias *every day*
tomar *to take*
tomaste ...? *have you taken ...?*
tonto *dizzy*
trabalha *you work*
trabalhador/a *hard-working*
trabalho *I work*
transeunte (o) *passer-by*
travões (os) *brakes*
tripas (as) *tripe*
triplicado/a *triplicate*
trocar *to change*
trovoadas (as) *thunder*
tudo *everything*

um pouco *a bit*
um pouco de *a bit of*
uma vez por ... *once a ...*
único/a *only*
universidade (a) *university*

vagas (as) *spaces*
vago/a *free*
vários/as *various*
vaso (o) *vase*
velho/a *old*
vende *sells*
vende-se *for sale*
vento (o) *wind*
ver *to see, watch*
verão (o) *summer*
vestido (o) *dress*
viagem (a) *journey*
vida (a) *life*
vidro (o) *window, glass*
vir *to come*
vista (a) *view*
vive *he/she/it/you live(s)*
vomitar *to be sick*

xarope (o) *syrup, remedy*

English–Portuguese vocabulary

a bit   um pouco
a bit of   um pouco de
a little bit   um pouquinho
able (to be)   poder
above   em cima
accept (to)   aceitar
address   a morada
aeroplane   o avião
afternoon   a tarde
against   contra
age   a idade
agreeable   agradável
air   o ar
airport   o aeroporto
alone   só, sozinho/a
also   também
always   sempre
and   e
apartment   o apartamento
are you well?   está bem?
armchair   a poltrona
arrange (to)   arranjar
arrive (to)   chegar
artistic   artístico/a
ask for (to)   pedir
aspirin   a aspirina
at least   pelo menos
atmosphere   o ambiente
attractions   as atracções
autumn   o outono
avenue   a avenida

back (at the)   ao fundo
balcony   o terraço
bank   o banco
bank clerk   o/a banqueiro/a
bathroom   a casa de banho
be (to)   ser / estar
beach   a praia
bean stew   a feijoada
because   porque
bed   a cama
bedroom   o quarto
behind   detrás (de)
believe (to)   crer
below   em baixo
bicycle   a bicicleta
big   grande
bigger   maior
blouse   a blusa
boat   o barco
boiled ham   o fiambre
book   o livro
bookcase   a estante
boot   a bota
boring   aborrecido/a
boss   o / a chefe
bottle   a garrafa
boyfriend   o namorado
brakes   os travões
bread   o pão
break-down   a avaria
broken   partido/a

broken down   avariado/a
brother   o irmão
building   o prédio, o edifício
bus   o autocarro
bus stop   a paragem (de autocarros)
bus terminus   o terminal
business   a empresa
busy (place)   movimentado/a
but   mas
butter   a manteiga
buy (to)   comprar

cake shop   a pastelaria
calm   calmo/a
camera   a máquina fotográfica
campsite   o parque de campismo
camper-van   o carro-cama
car   o carro, o automóvel
caravan   a caravana
careful   cuidado
carrot   a cenoura
cash desk   a caixa
cat   o gato
catch (to), bus etc.   apanhar
centre   o centro
change (to)   trocar, cambiar
charming   charmoso/a, encantador/ora
cheap   barato/a
cheese   o queijo
chicken   o frango, a galinha
child   a criança
church   a igreja
city   a cidade
clean   limpo/a
clean (to)   limpar
climate   o clima
clothes   a roupa
coach   a camioneta
collection   a colecção
colour   a cor
company   a companhia, a empresa

completely   completamente
cooker   o fogão
cooled   fresco/a
corner   a esquina
correct   certo/a
cost (to)   custar
country   o país
countryside   o campo
couple   o casal
cuisine   a cozinha
cultural   cultural
culture   a cultura
cupboard   o armário
customer   o / a freguês/esa

dangerous   perigoso/a
daughter   a filha
delicious   delicioso/a
Denmark   a Dinamarca
dentist   o / a dentista
depart (to)   partir
dessert   a sobremesa
diesel   o gasóleo
difficult   difícil
dining room   a sala de jantar
dirty   sujo/a
dizzy   tonto/a
do (to)   fazer
doctor   o / a médico/a
door   a porta
double room   o quarto de casal
downstairs   em baixo
dozen   a dúzia
dress   o vestido
drip (to)   pingar
drive (to)   conduzir
during   durante

early   cedo
easy   fácil
eat (to)   comer
egg   o ovo
either ... or ...   ou ... ou ...
elegant   elegante

English inglês/esa
espresso coffee o café, a bica
every cada
every day cada dia, todos os dias
every night cada noite, todas as noites
everyday quotidiano/a
everything tudo
exactly exactamente
excuse me desculpe!
exit a saída
expensive caro/a

faint (to) desmaiar
family a família
family (as a) em família
fashion house a casa de moda
fast rápido/a
father o pai
feel (to) sentir-(se)
few times poucas vezes
fill (to) encher
fill in (to) preencher
fireplace a lareira
first primeiro/a
floor (in block) o andar
flower a flor
food a comida
foot (on) (a) pé
for sale vende-se
for us para nós
form a ficha, o formulário
fortnight quinze dias
France a França
free livre, grátis
free time o tempo livre
fridge o frigorífico
friend o / a amigo/a
front (in ... of) em frente de
fruit juice o sumo
full of cheio/a de

generally geralmente, em geral

get to know (to) conhecer
girlfriend a namorada
glass (material) o vidro
go (to) ir
golf course o campo de golfe
Greece a Grécia
groceries as mercearias
guest house a pensão

half a kilo meio quilo
hard-working trabalhador/ora
have (to) ter
health a saúde
healthy saudável
heating o aquecimento
help a ajuda
here aqui, cá
high heeled de salto alto
highway a estrada
historical histórico/a
hole o buraco
holidays as férias
Holland a Holanda
honest honesto/a
horse o cavalo
hostel, inn o albergue
hotel o hotel
house a casa
housewife a dona de casa
how about? que tal?
how are you? como está?
how many? quantos/as?
how much is it? quanto é?
hunger a fome
husband o marido

I eu
I'm fine estou bem, óptimo/a
I'm well estou bem
ideal ideal
if se
improve (to) melhorar
in em, dentro
in between entre

in order to para
including incluindo
information a informação
interesting interessante
is é, está
island a ilha
isolated isolado/a

jacket a jaqueta
Japan o Japão
journey a viagem

kale soup o caldo verde
kilo o quilo
kitchen a cozinha

lake o lago
land a terra
later mais tarde
lawyer o / a advogado/a
lazy preguiçoso/a
leather o cabedal, o couro
leave (to), depart partir
left (on the) à esquerda
leisure time o tempo de lazer
letter a carta
library a biblioteca
life a vida
lift (car) a boleia
lift (elevator) o ascensor, o
  elevador
lift, tow o reboque
like (to) gostar de
likewise igualmente
list a lista
listen to (to) escutar
litre o litro
live (to) viver, morar
living room a sala de estar
London Londres
lonely solitário/a
long way (a) longe
lot (a) muito

magazine a revista
make (to) fazer
map o mapa
may I? posso?
meals as refeições
meat a carne
medicine o remédio, a medicina
meeting a reunião
menu a lista, a ementa
milk o leite
milky coffee o galão
modern moderno/a
money o dinheiro
more or less mais ou menos
more than mais de / que
mosquito o mosquito
mother a mãe
mud a lama
museum o museu
music a música
my name is chamo-me, o meu
  nome é …

name o nome
near perto
nearby (aqui) perto
need (to) precisar de
nervous nervoso/a
never nunca
newspaper o jornal
next to ao lado de
next year o ano próximo
nice (person) simpático/a
no não
noise o barulho
noisy barulhento/a
not não
now agora, já
number o número
nurse o / a enfermeiro/a

object o objecto
of course claro
offer (to) oferecer

office o escritório	*port* o porto
often muitas vezes	*portion* a dose, a porção
oil o óleo	*Portuguese* português/esa
old velho/a, antigo/a	*post office* o(s) correio(s)
olive oil o azeite	*postcard* o postal
on em	*pound* a libra
once a ... uma vez ...	*prefer (to)* preferir
only só	*pretty* bonito/a, lindo/a
opportunity a oportunidade	*price* o preço
orange a laranja	*probably* provavelmente
organize (to) organizar	*problem* o problema
others (the) os outros	*protection* a protecção
out there lá fora	*proud* orgulhoso/a
outside fora	*puncture* o furo
outskirts (on the) nos arredores	*purse* a carteira, o porta-
oven o forno	moedas
	put (to) pôr
packet o pacote	
pain, drag a maçada	*quality* a qualidade
paint (to) pintar	*quiet* sossegado/a
pair o par	*quite* bastante
parents os pais	
park o parque	*rain* a chuva
parked estacionado/a	*read (to)* ler
pass (to) passar	*reception* a recepção
passer-by o transeunte	*recommend (to)* recomendar
passport o passaporte	*region* a região
pear a pêra	*relaxing* relaxante
people as pessoas, a gente	*report (to)* comunicar
per night por noite	*reserve (to)* reservar
perhaps talvez	*reserved* reservado/a
personally pessoalmente	*retired* reformado/a
petrol a gasolina	*return (ticket)* ida e volta
phone booth a cabine telefónica	*right (on the)* à direita
phonecall a chamada	*right there* mesmo ali
picnic o pique-nique	*ripe* maduro/a
picture o quadro	*road* a rua
pill o comprimido	*road (main)* a estrada
place o lugar	*road sign* o sinal
platform a linha, a plataforma	*room* o quarto, a sala
play (to) (games) jogar	*roundabout* a rotunda
please se faz favor, por favor	
please ... faz favor de ...	*salt* o sal
pleased to meet you muito prazer	*salted cod* o bacalhau

sand   a areia
sandal   a sandália
sandwich   a sandes, sanduíche
sardine   a sardinha
Saturdays (on)   (aos / nos) sábados
say (to)   dizer
school   a escola
sea   o mar
seafood   o marisco
seafood rice   o arroz de marisco
see (to)   ver
see you soon   até breve, logo
seldom   raramente
sell (to)   vender
serious   sério/a
shade   a sombra
shirt   a camisa
shoe   o sapato
shop   a loja
shopping   as compras
shower   o chuveiro, o duche
sick (to be)   vomitar
sign (to)   assinar
single (ticket)   ida
sister   a irmã
sit down (to)   sentar-se
size   o tamanho, o número
skirt   a saia
sky   o céu
sleep (to)   dormir
small   pequeno/a
smoked ham   o presunto
snow   a neve
so, thus   assim
soap-opera   a telenovela
sofa   o sofá
soft drink   o refrigerante
someone   alguém
something   alguma coisa
sometimes   algumas vezes, de vez em quando
son   o filho
sorry (to be)   sentir, lamentar

space   o espaço
Spain   a Espanha
Spanish   espanhol/ola
speak (to)   falar
spend time (to)   passar
sports   os desportos
sporty   desportivo/a
spring   a primavera
square   a praça
stamp   o selo
station   a estação
stay, be situated (to)   ficar
stroll (to)   passear
student   o / a estudante
stung   picado/a
style   o estilo, o padrão
suit   o fato
summer   o verão
sunbathe (to)   apanhar, tomar sol
swim (to)   nadar
swimming pool   a piscina
Switzerland   a Suíça
symptom   a sintoma
syrup   o xarope

table   a mesa
take (to) (ingest)   tomar
take (to)   levar
taste (to)   provar
taxi   o táxi
teacher   o / a professor/ora
television   a televisão
tennis court   a quadra de ténis
tent   a tenda
thank you   obrigado/a
that   aquele/a
that thing   aquilo
theft   o roubo
then, after   depois
there   lá, ali
there is, are   há
there was, were   havia, houve
therefore   portanto

thing a coisa
third terceiro/a
this este/esta
thunder as trovoadas
ticket o bilhete
tie a gravata
till a caixa
today hoje
top (on ... of) em cima de
town a cidade
town plan a planta (da cidade)
trailer o atrelado
train o comboio
tree a árvore
tripe as tripas
triplicate triplicado/a
trousers as calças
try (to) provar
try on (to) experimentar
typical típico/a

underneath debaixo
unemployed desempregado/a
university a universidade
unpleasant desagradável
until, up to até
upstairs lá em cima

various vários/as
vase o vaso
very muito
very well muito bem
view a vista

wall a parede
wallet a carteira
want (to) querer
wardrobe o armário
washing machine a máquina de
 lavar roupa
watch (to) ver
way o caminho

well bem
well now! ora bem!
well then pois
wet molhado/a
what else? que mais?
what is it like? como é?
which? qual?
who? quem?
whole inteiro/a
wife a mulher, esposa
wind o vento
window a janela
winter o inverno
with com
with us connosco
without sem
wonderful maravilhoso/a
work (to), person trabalhar
work (to), things funcionar
writer o / a escritor/ora

year o ano
yes sim
yesterday ontem
young jovem

um (uma)	1	vinte e um (uma)	21
dois (duas)	2	trinta	30
três	3	quarenta	40
quatro	4	cinquenta	50
cinco	5	sessenta	60
seis	6	setenta	70
sete	7	oitenta	80
oito	8	noventa	90
nove	9	cem (cento)	100
dez	10	cento e um (uma)	101
onze	11	duzentos/as	200
doze	12	trezentos/as	300
treze	13	quatrocentos/as	400
catorze	14	quinhentos/as	500
quinze	15	seiscentos/as	600
dezasseis	16	setecentos/as	700
dezassete	17	oitocentos/as	800
dezoito	18	novecentos/as	900
dezanove	19	mil	1,000
vinte	20	un milhão	1,000,000

primeiro/a, 1°/1ª	*first*
segundo/a, 2°/2ª	*second*
terceiro/a, 3°/3ª	*third*
quarto/a, 4°/4ª	*fourth*
quinto/a, 5°/5ª	*fifth*

sexto/a, 6°/6ª	*sixth*
sétimo/a, 7°/7ª	*seventh*
oitavo/a, 8°/8ª	*eighth*
nono/a, 9°/9ª	*ninth*
décimo/a, 10°/10ª	*tenth*

grammar index

teach
yourself

portuguese
manuela cook

- Do you want to cover the basics then progress fast?
- Do you want to communicate in a range of situations?
- Do you want to reach a high standard?

Portuguese starts with the basics but moves at a lively pace to give you a good level of understanding, speaking and writing. You will have lots of opportunity to practise the kind of language you will need to be able to communicate with confidence and understand the cultures of speakers of Portuguese.

portuguese conversation
sue tyson-ward

teach yourself

- Do you want to talk with confidence?
- Are you looking for basic conversation skills?
- Do you want to understand what people say to you?

Portuguese Conversation is a three-hour, all-audio course which you can use at any time, whether you want a quick refresher before a trip or whether you are a complete beginner. The 20 dialogues on CDs 1 and 2 will teach you the Portuguese you will need to speak and understand, without getting bogged down with grammar. CD 3, uniquely, teaches skills for listening and understanding. This is the perfect accompaniment to **Beginner's Portuguese** and **Portugese** in the **teach yourself** range: www.teachyourself.co.uk.

| teach yourself | **portuguese grammar**
sue tyson-ward |

- Are you looking for an accessible guide to Portuguese grammar?
- Do you want a book you can use either as a reference or as a course?
- Would you like exercises to reinforce your learning?

Portuguese Grammar explains the most important structures in a clear and jargon-free way, with plenty of examples to show how they work in context. Use the book as a comprehensive reference to dip in and out or work through it to build your knowledge.

brazilian portuguese
sue tyson-ward

- Do you want to cover the basics then progress fast?
- Do you want to communicate in a range of situations?
- Do you want to reach a high standard?

Brazilian Portuguese starts with the basics but moves at a lively pace to give you a good level of understanding, speaking and writing. You will have lots of opportunity to practise the kind of language you will need to be able to communicate with confidence and understand Brazilian culture.

teach yourself®

From Advanced Sudoku to Zulu, you'll find everything you need in the **teach yourself** range, in books, on CD and on DVD.

Visit **www.teachyourself.co.uk** for more details.

Advanced Sudoku and Kakuro
Afrikaans
Alexander Technique
Algebra
Ancient Greek
Applied Psychology
Arabic
Arabic Conversation
Aromatherapy
Art History
Astrology
Astronomy
AutoCAD 2004
AutoCAD 2007
Ayurveda
Baby Massage and Yoga
Baby Signing
Baby Sleep
Bach Flower Remedies
Backgammon
Ballroom Dancing
Basic Accounting
Basic Computer Skills
Basic Mathematics
Beauty
Beekeeping
Beginner's Arabic Script
Beginner's Chinese Script
Beginner's Dutch

Beginner's French
Beginner's German
Beginner's Greek
Beginner's Greek Script
Beginner's Hindi
Beginner's Hindi Script
Beginner's Italian
Beginner's Japanese
Beginner's Japanese Script
Beginner's Latin
Beginner's Mandarin Chinese
Beginner's Portuguese
Beginner's Russian
Beginner's Russian Script
Beginner's Spanish
Beginner's Turkish
Beginner's Urdu Script
Bengali
Better Bridge
Better Chess
Better Driving
Better Handwriting
Biblical Hebrew
Biology
Birdwatching
Blogging
Body Language
Book Keeping
Brazilian Portuguese

Bridge
British Citizenship Test, The
British Empire, The
British Monarchy from Henry VIII, The
Buddhism
Bulgarian
Bulgarian Conversation
Business French
Business Plans
Business Spanish
Business Studies
C++
Calculus
Calligraphy
Cantonese
Caravanning
Car Buying and Maintenance
Card Games
Catalan
Chess
Chi Kung
Chinese Medicine
Christianity
Classical Music
Coaching
Cold War, The
Collecting
Computing for the Over 50s
Consulting
Copywriting
Correct English
Counselling
Creative Writing
Cricket
Croatian
Crystal Healing
CVs
Czech
Danish
Decluttering
Desktop Publishing
Detox
Digital Home Movie Making
Digital Photography
Dog Training
Drawing

Dream Interpretation
Dutch
Dutch Conversation
Dutch Dictionary
Dutch Grammar
Eastern Philosophy
Electronics
English as a Foreign Language
English Grammar
English Grammar as a Foreign Language
Entrepreneurship
Estonian
Ethics
Excel 2003
Feng Shui
Film Making
Film Studies
Finance for Non-Financial Managers
Finnish
First World War, The
Fitness
Flash 8
Flash MX
Flexible Working
Flirting
Flower Arranging
Franchising
French
French Conversation
French Dictionary
French for Homebuyers
French Grammar
French Phrasebook
French Starter Kit
French Verbs
French Vocabulary
Freud
Gaelic
Gaelic Conversation
Gaelic Dictionary
Gardening
Genetics
Geology
German
German Conversation

German Grammar
German Phrasebook
German Starter Kit
German Vocabulary
Globalization
Go
Golf
Good Study Skills
Great Sex
Green Parenting
Greek
Greek Conversation
Greek Phrasebook
Growing Your Business
Guitar
Gulf Arabic
Hand Reflexology
Hausa
Herbal Medicine
Hieroglyphics
Hindi
Hindi Conversation
Hinduism
History of Ireland, The
Home PC Maintenance and
  Networking
How to DJ
How to Run a Marathon
How to Win at Casino Games
How to Win at Horse Racing
How to Win at Online Gambling
How to Win at Poker
How to Write a Blockbuster
Human Anatomy & Physiology
Hungarian
Icelandic
Improve Your French
Improve Your German
Improve Your Italian
Improve Your Spanish
Improving Your Employability
Indian Head Massage
Indonesian
Instant French
Instant German
Instant Greek
Instant Italian

Instant Japanese
Instant Portuguese
Instant Russian
Instant Spanish
Internet, The
Irish
Irish Conversation
Irish Grammar
Islam
Israeli-Palestinian Conflict, The
Italian
Italian Conversation
Italian for Homebuyers
Italian Grammar
Italian Phrasebook
Italian Starter Kit
Italian Verbs
Italian Vocabulary
Japanese
Japanese Conversation
Java
JavaScript
Jazz
Jewellery Making
Judaism
Jung
Kama Sutra, The
Keeping Aquarium Fish
Keeping Pigs
Keeping Poultry
Keeping a Rabbit
Knitting
Korean
Latin
Latin American Spanish
Latin Dictionary
Latin Grammar
Letter Writing Skills
Life at 50: For Men
Life at 50: For Women
Life Coaching
Linguistics
LINUX
Lithuanian
Magic
Mahjong
Malay